THE VERY BEST OF
Children's Book
Illustration

Compiled by the Society of Illustrators

NORTH
LIGHT
BOOKS

Cincinnati, Ohio

97 96 95 94 93   5 4 3 2 1

Library of Congress Cataloging in Publication Data

The very best of children's book illustration / compiled by the Society of
     Illustrators.
          p.   cm.
     Exhibition held Oct. 21 through Nov. 27, 1992 in the galleries of
the Society of Illustrators, New York City.
     ISBN 0-89134-540-X
     1. Illustrated books, Children's—United States—Exhibitions.
2. Illustration of books—20th century—United States—Exhibitions.
I. Society of Illustrators (New York, N.Y.)
NC975.V45   1993
741.6'42'09730747471—dc20   93-10484
                                                                       CIP

Sources for the front cover art are as follows:
top left —*The Fortune-Tellers* (illustrated by Trina Schart Hyman);
top right —*The Flyaway Girl* (written and illustrated by Ann Grifalconi);
middle left — *The Lost Sailor* (illustrated by Richard Egielski);
middle right — *June 29, 1999* (written and illustrated by David Weisner);
bottom left — *Asleep, Asleep* (illustrated by Nancy Tafuri);
bottom right — *Zomo the Rabbit* (written and illustrated by Gerald McDermott).

Edited by Lynn Haller
Designed by Sandy Conopeotis

The permissions beginning on page 130 constitute an extension of this copyright page.

Acknowledgments

Dilys Evans and the Society of Illustrators would like to acknowledge the contribution of the following Original Art Exhibition organizers and committee members, past and present: Anne Childs, Alan E. Cober, Pat Cummings, Diane Dillon, Susanne Dooley, Gregory Etheart, Kathleen O'Conor Finn, Charlotte Freihofer, Layne Taylor Gandy, Barbara Genco, Marion Hanes, Pam Hastings, Diane Hess, Allyn Johnston, Jill Kastner, Sue Kellman, Marcia Leonard, Ted Lewin, Joanna Long, Wendell Minor, Dick Morrill, Sheila Paterson, Jerry Pinkney, Diane Roback, Charles Santore, Peter Sis, Lane Smith, David Wiesner.

From the exhibition "The Original Art 1992," held in the galleries of the Society of
Illustrators Museum of American Illustration, 128 East 63rd Street, New York
City, from October 21 through November 25, 1992.

Dedication

John Donovan, Children's Book Council President

As chief staff officer of the Children's Book Council from 1967 until his death on April 29, 1992, John Donovan was a major voice in the development of children's book publishing in the United States.

His strong advocacy of an international community of people devoted to children and their literature reflected his belief that books have a direct and profound influence on children's intellectual and emotional lives and that it is the responsibility of publishers to overcome limitations of geography and ideological differences to produce the best possible materials for children.

In the late sixties and early seventies he encouraged U.S. publishers to explore new ways of reaching children through the classrooms and bookstores as well as libraries.

Donovan was the author of five books for young people, including the groundbreaking *I'll Get There. It Better Be Worth the Trip*, *Family*, and *Wild in the World*. His play, *Riverside Drive,* was produced in New York in 1963.

For his work for IBBYP (International Board for Books for Young People) he was awarded the Jella Lepman Medal in 1991 for his unique contribution in the development of the Board.

John Donovan was also a poet and a scholar with a keen eye for beauty and a wicked sense of humor. He was a gentle man but wild in his passion for the arts. He was a shoulder to lean on when the idea for a lavish exhibition featuring children's book illustration was first proposed. Through the years he was a stalwart supporter of the event.

Dedicated to John Donovan from Every Child

TERI SLOTKIN

Contents

Illustrator: Donald Crews

Author: Donald Crews

Publisher: Greenwillow Books

Interior illustration from
Shortcut.

Watercolor and gouache, 8¹/₄" x 20"

Foreword

This year's Original Art Exhibition is much like a story book. It has its beginnings somewhere in a gallery in New York City, and now finds its home at the prestigious Society of Illustrators. The cast of characters: A jury that includes some of the best working in children's literature. To them I give my thanks for their diligence and hard work. The plot: Which books will be chosen to represent the best in children's book illustration for 1992? The awarding of medals and the inclusion of the winners in this book is a fitting end to this exciting story.

The children's book artist has a number of responsibilities aside from filling space and relaying the writer's plot when illustrating a story—most important, he or she is responsible to the creative self and to children. And we, as illustrators of children's books, are privileged to have an audience that matches our own imaginations.

What you see here is but a sampling of the creative work being done today. I am pleased and excited to be a part of this industry and an exhibition that speaks to the best in children's literature today. This book is a record and celebration of just that.

Jerry Pinkney

Jerry Pinkney
Chairman, The Original Art 1992

The Society of Illustrators, founded in 1901, has since its earliest days dedicated its major energies to fulfilling its mission: the promotion and stimulation of interest in the art of illustration.

Throughout the years, exhibitions covering all areas of our profession have been held by the Society of Illustrators. The prestigious Annual Exhibition and subsequent Annual Book presents the Advertising, Editorial, Book and Institutional categories. Exhibitions within specialized areas of illustration have been staged as well.

"The Original Art," the annual juried exhibition for the best of children's book illustration, has been exhibited in the galleries of the Society of Illustrators' Museum of American Illustration for the past three years. This edition is the first published compilation of that show. The enormous range and technical diversity of this genre makes this book especially appealing. We hope it will be the first of many to come.

Eileen Hedy Schultz
President, Society of Illustrators

The Original Art Exhibition: Its Beginnings

The Original Art Exhibition really began as an idea in the seventies, when I was working for *Cricket*, a magazine for children. *Cricket* brought me into contact with many of the leading children's book illustrators and with their original art. This association triggered a quest into the realm of children's picture books—a journey that would affect not only my career but my life.

My artistic training helped me to realize that this new world of pictures was actually the fine art of children's book illustration. When the time came to leave *Cricket* and move back to New York, I knew that somehow I would pursue this concept, possibly in the form of an annual exhibition of the original art from children's books.

I always knew that I would write about this intriguing new world, but I needed other believers to take the next step. Marcia Leonard, whom I first met as an editor at *Cricket*, was the first and most important colleague to join me. Currently a publicist of children's books and their creators, Marcia was a natural, and she shared the passion needed for such an endeavor. Dick Morrill, a teacher of illustration and a sculptor, came next; he too shared our vision and determination to give the art of children's books higher visibility.

After months of searching and endless presentations, Dick Morrill suggested that I call the Master Eagle Gallery on West 25th Street. I went to see them, made one final presentation, and they agreed that such an exhibition would be perfect for them, especially in their role as a nonprofit organization wanting to attract the community.

In 1980 very few galleries represented contemporary children's book illustrators, and there was no major exhibition of the size and nature of The Original Art Exhibition. So here, for the first time, would be the opportunity to see original art that historically received very little attention after it had been returned from the printer. It was also an opportunity to consider the work of the children's book illustrator as an art form.

From its inception I wanted this exhibition to be a place where the entire community of children's book people could come together once a year to celebrate "The Very Best of Children's Book Illustration." We opened the exhibition to members of the Children's Book Council; in this way, the volunteer committee could consider the publishing catalogs of each house and ensure every publisher a place in the exhibition.

The committee was comprised of art directors, editors, children's book librarians, reviewers and illustrators, all of whom were a part of this unique industry and understood it. By making the books themselves part of the exhibit, we were able to emphasize the importance of reading and draw

The first show (1980), left to right: Dick Morrill, Clarence Baylis, Al Mauro, Herbert Rickman (Special Assistant to then Mayor Edward Koch), Marcia Leonard and Dilys Evans…at the Master Eagle Galleries

an audience that included a great many children. Illustrators came to see each other's work and to get the feel of the current year in publishing, art directors came seeking new talent, and the public came to see some of the best work created for children and to identify the book for purchase later.

November 19, 1980 was opening night, and the beginning of eight fruitful years of holding the Original Art Exhibition at the Master Eagle Gallery under the watchful eye of Public Relations Director Clarence Baylis. The Master Eagle family of companies was our gracious host until it was purchased by another company. As a direct result of the purchase, one of the two galleries became office space, leaving just one gallery to continue. It was now 1988; that year there was no exhibition, and I began to look around for another space. Meanwhile the publishing community was tremendously supportive and encouraging as its members realized that the Original Art Exhibition had become a part of their annual calendar and part of their lives.

The Society of Illustrators, with its prestigious reputation in the publishing world, seemed a perfect home for an exhibition of this caliber. The idea was presented to the Museum Committee for consideration and was accepted. For this first exhibition in 1989, the Society agreed to let us rent both galleries of the Society of Illustrators' Museum of American Illustration while they provided backup for the details and printing needs. The exhibition was so successful that in 1990 the Society accepted it as an annual event on its calendar. We had found a home in a place that represented illustrators and their work. The quest was over.

The publication of this book is another milestone in making this remarkable art form accessible to everyone. In acknowledging the past of children's book illustration and documenting its present and future, it becomes a great reference not only for those with a professional interest in the tradition of picture books, but for those who simply love good pictures.

Dilys Evans
Founder, The Original Art Exhibition

The Original Art Exhibition: 1992 Selection Process

The Society of Illustrators begins work on The Original Art Exhibition nine months before it is scheduled to open its doors to the public in the fall. The Chair is chosen based on knowledge of the industry as a whole, the willingness to give as much time as is required to steer the process to its conclusion, and the ability to keep an open mind when dealing with an art form that has such an enormous diversity and audience age range. The Chair plays a pivotal role during jury selection, at which time he or she must carefully balance the backgrounds of jury members so that together the jury reflects the entire children's book publishing scene.

The "Call for Entries" consists of a mailing to artists, art directors, publishers, editors, members of the Society of Illustrators and nonmembers to submit their published books for consideration.

All books must first comply with the criteria for entry. They must be copyrighted in the same year the exhibition is held, and published in the United States; no foreign entries are allowed. Two categories of books are eligible: picture books and chapter books. Picture books must have at least one illustration per spread and chapter books at least one picture for each chapter. No textbooks, jackets or young adult books are accepted for consideration.

Once it has been established that the books meet these entry criteria, they are processed and made ready for the jury, which in 1992 consisted of eight members. After receiving judging guidelines from the Chair, each juror casts his or her vote on the entry form itself, with each juror using a different color of marker so that his or her progress can be tracked during the course of the day. A simple in-or-out system is used and the books are laid in piles on tables that line the gallery walls. When all eight jury members are finished judging, the results are processed by the Society staff.

At all times the jury must keep in mind that in the world of children's books, art created for the very young might seem very simple by comparison with that created for the older age levels, and vote accordingly.

The jury then selects the winners of the Gold and Silver medals for the best in full-color and the best in black and white. There is open discussion and armed with colored discs, each juror finally votes the medal.

1992 Chairman and Jury

Jerry Pinkney, an award-winning illustrator of children's books, has been honored for the body of his work with a Citation for Children's Literature from Drexel University, and with the David McCord Children's Literature Citation from Framingham State College. He has also received the Alumni Award for 1992 from the Philadelphia College of Art and Design, and has his work exhibited at the Indianapolis Museum of Art, Cornell University and the University of Delaware. A traveling exhibition of his paintings has been displayed at the Philadelphia Afro-American Historical and Cultural Museum, the Schomburg Center for Black Culture in New York City, and at the University at Buffalo, SUNY, where Mr. Pinkney was Visiting Professor in the Department of Art.

Alan E. Cober has received eleven medals from the Society of Illustrators, was twice named on *The New York Times* Ten Best Illustrated Books list, and is Professor of Art and Distinguished Visiting Artist, University at Buffalo, SUNY.

Pat Cummings has illustrated seventeen books, authored four and compiled the book *Talking with Artists*. Pat received the Coretta Scott King Award for *My Momma Needs Me*, featured on "Reading Rainbow."

Ted Lewin has illustrated over 100 titles and authored six of his own.

Joanna Long, reviewer, is currently the Y.A. Children's Book Editor for Kirkus Reviews, New York.

Charles Santore has received both an Award of Excellence and the Hamilton King Award from the Society of Illustrators, received the Alumni Award from the Philadelphia College of Art, and has illustrated *Aesop's Fables*, *Tales of Peter Rabbit* and *The Wizard of Oz*.

Peter Sis has illustrated over twenty books internationally, was named three times on *The New York Times* Ten Best Illustrated Books list, and received the Golden Bear at the Berlin Film Festival for the animated film *Heads*.

Lane Smith was named on *The New York Times* Ten Best Illustrated Books list for his first book. He received four medals from the Society of Illustrators and received the Golden Apple from the Biennale of Illustration Bratislava.

David Wiesner, author and illustrator, received the Caldecott Honor in 1989 for *Freefall* and the 1992 Caldecott Medal for his wordless fantasy, *Tuesday*.

1992 Award Winners

Above

1992 Gold Medalist

Illustrators: Leo and Diane Dillon

Author: Nancy White Carlstrom

Publisher: Philomel Books

Interior illustration from *Northern Lullaby*, the tale of an Alaskan child who says goodnight to the natural world and all those who occupy it.

Pastel-watercolor on bristolboard, 11½" x 20½"

Above right

1992 Gold Medalist

Illustrator: Richard McGuire

Author: Richard McGuire

Publisher: Rizzoli International Publications

Interior illustration from *The Orange Book*, a picture book recounting the story of fourteen oranges as they make their way in the world.

Gouache and pencil, 11½" x 21½"

Right

1992 Silver Medalist

Illustrator: William Joyce

Author: William Joyce

Publisher: HarperCollins

Interior illustration from *Bently & egg*, a springtime comedy celebrating new life, friendship and fatherhood.

Acrylic, 9" x 17"

The Finalists

Above

Illustrator: Robert Roth

Author: Sheron Williams

Publisher: Atheneum Publishers

Interior illustration from *And in the Beginning...*, an adaptation of an African-American creation tale.

Watercolor, 15¹/₂″ x 24¹/₂″

Right

Illustrator: Rosemary Wells

Author: Rosemary Wells

Publisher: Dial Books for Young Readers

Interior illustration from *The Island Light*, one of the three Voyage to the Bunny Planet books about a utopia headed by a bunny queen.

Watercolor and sepia ink, 7″ x 7″

Illustrator: Kimberly Bulcken Root

Author: Eric A. Kimmel

Publisher: Holiday House

Cover and interior illustration from *Boots and His Brothers*, the retelling of a Norwegian folktale about a young man's kindness to an old beggar woman, and how that kindness is rewarded.

Pen and ink and watercolor, 11" x 8½"

Below

Illustrator: John O'Brien

Author: Judith Ross Enderle and Stephanie Gordon Tessler

Publisher: Boyds Mills Press

Interior illustration from *Six Creepy Sheep*, the story of how six sheep in ghost costumes encounter other costumed animals on their way to a Halloween party.

Pen and ink, watercolor and dyes, 9½" x 19"

Left

Illustrator: Trina Schart Hyman

Author: Lloyd Alexander

Publisher: E.P. Dutton Children's Books

Interior illustration from *The Fortune-Tellers*, an original fable involving mistaken identity and an ironic twist of fate, set in the northern province of Cameroon, West Africa.

Ink, acrylic and crayon, 8³/₄" x 22"

Below

Illustrator: Daniel San Souci

Author: Robert D. San Souci

Publisher: Doubleday

Interior illustration from *Feathertop*, a retelling of the Nathaniel Hawthorne short story about a scarecrow turned into a man by a witch.

Watercolor, 14" x 15"

Illustrator: Chris Raschka
Author: Chris Raschka
Publisher: Orchard Books

Cover and interior illustration from *Charlie Parker Played Be Bop*, an introduction for children to the great saxophonist and his music.
Charcoal pencil and watercolor, 9″ x 9¼″

Above
Illustrator: Peggy Rathmann
Author: Barbara Bottner
Publisher: G.P. Putnam's Sons

Interior illustration from *Bootsie Barker Bites*, the story of a little girl who only wants to play games in which she bites, until her friend comes up with a better game.
Mixed media, 10½″ x 16″

Right
Illustrator: Wendell Minor
Author: Charlotte Zolotow
Publisher: HarperCollins

Cover and interior illustration from *The Seashore Book*, the tale of a mother and son and the story she tells him about the seashore.
Gouache and watercolor, 11¾″ x 9¼″

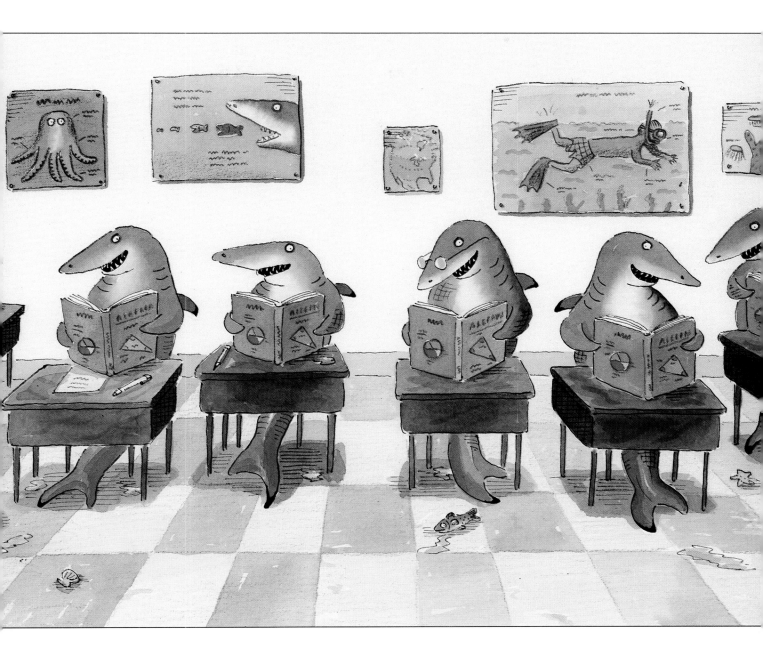

Above left

Illustrator: Denise Fleming

Author: Denise Fleming

Publisher: Henry Holt and Company

Interior illustration from *Count!*, a counting book where the numbers are presented by lively and colorful animals.

Pulp painting, 11" x 9"

Left

Illustrator: Leslie Baker

Author: Leslie Baker

Publisher: Little, Brown & Co.

Interior illustration from *The Antique Store Cat*, the story of Alice, a calico cat, who creates a stir when she makes an unauthorized visit to an antique shop.

Watercolor, 4¹/₂" x 7¹/₄"

Above

Illustrator: Paul Meisel

Author: Alvin Schwartz

Publisher: HarperCollins

Interior illustration from *Busy Buzzing Bumblebees*, an illustrated collection of forty-six tongue twisters.

Pen and ink, watercolor and pencil, 10¹/₂" x 14¹/₂"

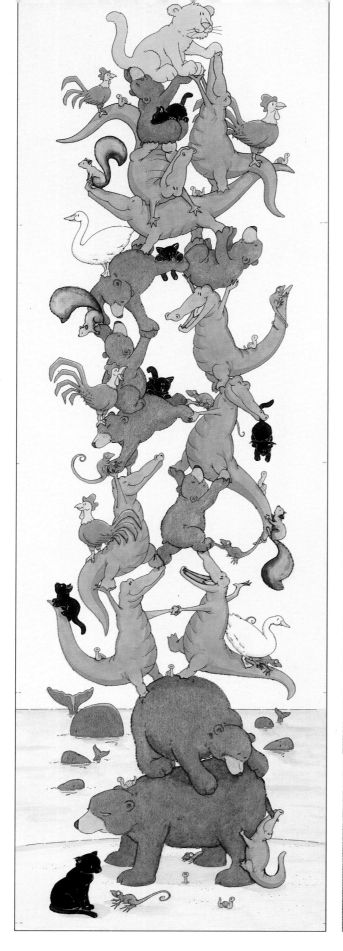

Illustrator: Matthew Van Fleet

Author: Matthew Van Fleet

Publisher: Dial Books for Young Readers

Interior illustration from *One Yellow Lion*, a fold-out counting book.

Watercolor and ink, 24" x 8"

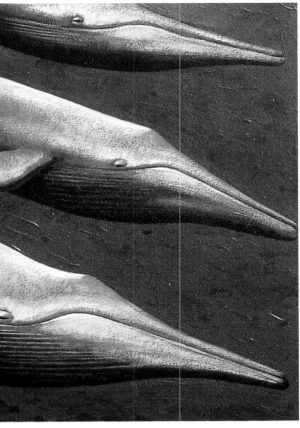

Illustrator: Lynne Russell
Author: Ann Marie Linden
Publisher: Dial Books for Young Readers

Interior illustration from *One Smiling Grandma*, a counting book set in the Caribbean.
Oil pastel, 9¾" x 19¾"

Illustrator: Leonard Everett Fisher
Author: Poems selected by Myra Cohn Livingston
Publisher: Holiday House

Cover and interior illustration from *If You Ever Meet a Whale*, an anthology of poetry, both commissioned and traditional, about whales.
Acrylic, 10" x 19"

Illustrator: Jacqueline Geis
Author: Jacqueline Geis
Publisher: Ideals Publishing Corporation

Cover illustration from *Where the Buffalo Roam*, an interpretation of the song "Home on the Range" adapting verses to include animals, plants and geographical features of the Southwest.

Watercolor, 6½" x 18½"

Left
Illustrator: Ted Lewin
Author: Corinne Demas Bliss
Publisher: Harcourt Brace Jovanovich

Cover and interior illustration from *Matthew's Meadow*, the tale of a boy who learns the magic and wisdom of the natural world from a red-tailed hawk.

Watercolor, 9" x 7"

Illustrator: Ann Grifalconi
Author: Ann Grifalconi
Publisher: Little, Brown & Co.

Interior illustration from *Flyaway Girl*, the story of a girl who is sent on an errand by her mother but encounters many distractions until the ancestor's spirits guide her on her way to becoming a wise little woman.

Mixed media photo collage, 13" x 17½"

Above
Illustrator: Jim LaMarche
Author: Laura Krauss Melmed
Publisher: Lothrop, Lee & Shepard

Cover and interior illustration from *The Rainbabies*, the tale of a childless couple whose care of the twelve babies the moon has bestowed on them results in an unexpected reward.
Watercolor, colored pencil and acrylic, 14" x 23"

Illustrator: Douglas Florian
Author: Douglas Florian
Publisher: Greenwillow Books

Interior illustration from *At the Zoo*, a book of couplets describing a day at the zoo.
Pen, sepia ink and colored pencil, 8⁷/₈" x 14"

Left
Illustrator: Frané Lessac
Author: Compiled by Irving Burgie
Publisher: Tambourine Books

Interior illustration from *Caribbean Carnival*, a picture book of Calypso songs that includes "Michael Row the Boat" and "Yellow Bird."
Gouache, 13" x 10"

Illustrator: David Shannon
Author: Rafe Martin
Publisher: Putnam

Interior illustration from *The Rough-Face Girl*, a Native
American version of the Cinderella folktale.
Acrylic, 17" x 13"

Below
Illustrator: Shonto Begay
Author: Traditional story retold by Shonto Begay
Publisher: Scholastic Inc.

Cover illustration from *Ma'ii and Cousin Horned Toad*, a
traditional Navaho folktale of how a conniving coyote is
taught a lesson by his cousin Horned Toad.
Watercolor and pencil, 12" x 16"

Illustrator: Jean and Mou-Sien Tseng

Author: Ryerson Johnson

Publisher: Simon & Schuster Books for
Young Readers

Interior illustration from *Kenji and the Magic
Geese*, the story of a goose that escapes
from a picture on a boy's wall.

Watercolor, 11" x 17"

Above

Illustrator: Petra Mathers

Author: Leah Komaiko

Publisher: Doubleday Books for Young Readers

Interior illustration from *Aunt Elaine Does the Dance from Spain*, the story of Aunt Elaine from Maine, who takes her niece to see her perform her Spanish dance.

Watercolor and pencil, 11½" x 14"

Left

Illustrator: Julie Downing

Author: Ursula K. LeGuin

Publisher: Orchard Books

Interior illustration from *A Ride on the Red Mare's Back*, an adaptation of a folktale about a girl who, with the aid of her magical wooden horse, rescues her brother, who was kidnapped by trolls.

Watercolor and colored pencil, 12" x 9"

Above

Illustrator: Ron Lightburn

Author: Sheryl McFarlane

Publisher: Orca Book Publishers

Interior illustration from *Waiting for the Whales*, the story of an old man who passes on to his granddaughter his love of nature and his passion for the whales that visit their cove each year.

Colored pencil, 15⅝" x 14"

Above

Illustrator: John O'Brien

Author: David F. Birchman

Publisher: Lothrop, Lee & Shepard

Interior illustration from *Brother Billy Bronto's Bygone Blues Band*, a rhyming story about a group of dinosaur musicians and how they became extinct.

Pen and ink, watercolor, and dyes, 11" x 17"

Right

Illustrator: Jacqueline Rogers

Author: Compiled by Dilys Evans

Publisher: Scholastic Inc.

Interior illustration from *Monster Soup*, an illustrated book of poems about monsters.

Watercolor, 17" x 24"

Above

Illustrator: Seymour Chwast

Author: Deborah Johnston

Publisher: Harcourt Brace
    Jovanovich

Interior illustration from
Mathew Michael's Beastly Day,
the story of a day in the life of
Mathew Michael, a boy who
changes into various animals
depending on his mood.
Marker and cello-tak, 9" x 19"

Illustrator: Vincent Nasta

Author: Jean Craighead George

Publisher: HarperCollins

Cover illustration from *The Moon of the Winter Bird*, a book that chronicles one year in the life of a sparrow.

Oil on Masonite, 14" x 11"

Illustrator: Catherine Stock

Author: Collected by Bernice Wolman

Publisher: Atheneum

Interior illustration from *Taking Turns*, a compilation of pairs of poems, one written for children and one for adults, on similar themes.

Watercolor on scratchboard, 10" x 5"

Below

Illustrator: Leslie Tryon

Author: Leslie Tryon

Publisher: Atheneum

Cover and interior illustration from *Albert's Play*, the story of a boy and the play he puts on.

Watercolor and Prismacolor pencil, 8¼" x 10¼"

Below

Illustrator: Kevin Hawkes

Author: Kevin Hawkes

Publisher: Lothrop, Lee & Shepard

Interior illustration from *His Royal Buckliness*, the story of a young boy who is kidnapped by giants and rescued by friends bearing gifts.

Acrylic, 13" x 22"

Left

Illustrator: David Catrow

Author: Robert Southey (1774-1843)

Publisher: Henry Holt and Company

Cover illustration from *The Cataract of Lodore*, an illustrated interpretation of Robert Southey's poem.

Ink and watercolor, 9½" x 30"

Below

Illustrator: Tomie dePaola

Author: Tomie dePaola

Publisher: G.P. Putnam's Sons

Interior illustration from *Jingle, the Christmas Clown*, the story of a clown and a troupe of baby animals who put on a special Christmas Eve show for an Italian village too poor to celebrate the holiday.

Acrylic on handmade paper, 15" x 22¼"

Below

Illustrator: Eric Beddows

Author: Barbara J. Esbensen

Publisher: HarperCollins

Interior illustration from *Who Shrank My Grandmother's House?*, a collection of poems of discovery.

Watercolor, gouache, pencil and colored pencil, 9½" x 7¼"

Left

Illustrator: Vladimir Radunsky

Authors: Eugenia and Vladimir Radunsky

Publisher: Henry Holt and Company

Cover and interior illustration from *Square Triangle Round Skinny*, a set of four shaped books and a poster.

Handcolored linoprint, 34¹⁄₄" x 8¹⁄₂"

Illustrator: Robert Bender

Author: Robert Bender

Publisher: Henry Holt and Company

Cover and interior illustration from *A Little Witch Magic*, the story of a little girl who visits a lonely witch on Halloween.

Vinyl on acetate, 10" x 16"

Illustrator: Troy Howell

Author: Amy Ehrlich

Publisher: Dial Books for Young Readers

Cover illustration from *Lucy's Winter Tale*, the story of a
little girl kidnapped by a juggler who includes the girl in
his search for his sweetheart.

Acrylic, 10" x 8"

Illustrator: David Johnson

Author: Retold by David Johnson

Publisher: Rabbit Ears Books/Picture Book
Studio

Interior illustration from *The Boy Who Drew Cats*, about how an obsession with drawing cats leads a boy to a mysterious experience.

Ink, watercolor and colored pencil, 11" x 15"

Below

Illustrator: Richard Egielski

Author: Pam Conrad

Publisher: HarperCollins

Interior illustration from *The Lost Sailor*, a picture book about a sailor, famed for his seamanship and luck, who is shipwrecked.

Watercolor, 10¼" x 12¾"

Illustrator: Paul Borovsky

Author: Retold by Gerda Mantinband

Publisher: Greenwillow Books

Cover and interior illustration from *Blabbermouths*, an adaptation of a German folktale about an innocent fool and his clever wife whose shrewdness saves their fortune.

Watercolor, colored pencil and ink, 5" x 5"

Illustrator: Victoria Chess

Author: Florence Parry Heide

Publisher: Lothrop, Lee & Shepard

Interior illustration from *Grim and Ghastly Goings-On*, an illustrated book of poems about monsters.

Watercolor and ink, 6" x 4½"

Illustrator: Jeanette Winter

Author: Selma Lagerlöf (1858-1940),
    translated by Susanna Marie Farrell
    Stevens

Publisher: Alfred A. Knopf

Interior illustration from *The Changeling*, the story, by Nobel Prize-winning author Selma Lagerlöf, of a mother whose young son is exchanged for a troll child, and how her love saves them both.

Acrylic, 7¾" x 6"

Above left
Illustrator: Marìa Cristina Brusca
Authors: Marìa Cristina Brusca and Tona
  Wilson
Publisher: Henry Holt and Company

Cover and interior illustration from *The
Blacksmith and the Devils*, an adaptation of
an Argentinian folktale about a blacksmith
who makes a deal with the devil to extend
his youth and good fortune.
Watercolor and ink, 10¼" x 16¼"

Left
Illustrator: Betsy Everitt
Author: Betsy Everitt
Publisher: Harcourt Brace Jovanovich

Interior illustration from *Mean Soup*, the
story of a boy and his mother who fill up a
soup with mean faces to stir away a bad day.
Gouache, 13" x 13"

Above
Illustrator: Rosekrans Hoffman
Author: Jane Yolen; musical arrangements
  by Adam Stemple
Publisher: Boyds Mills Press

Interior illustration from *Jane Yolen's Mother
Goose Songbook*, an illustrated interpretation of some of the traditional Mother Goose
songs.
Colored ink and pencil, 9" x 10"

Below

Illustrator: James Warhola

Author: Retold by Peggy Thomson

Publisher: Simon & Schuster

Cover illustration from *The Brave Little Tailor*, an adaptation of the classic Brothers Grimm tale of a tailor who outwits the king and wins half his kingdom.

Watercolor, 15" x 22"

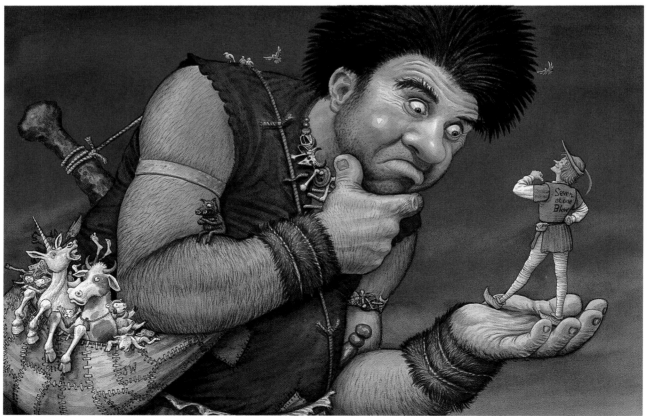

Illustrator: Henri Sorensen

Author: Anne Wescott Dodd

Publisher: Simon & Schuster Books for
Young Readers

Interior illustration from *Footprints and
Shadows*, a book that tells readers what
happens to footprints when snow melts and
shadows when they are dispelled by light.

Acrylic, 10" x 25"

Below

Illustrator: John Collier

Author: Retold by Vivian Werner

Publisher: Viking

Interior illustration from *Petrouchka*, a
retelling of the Stravinsky ballet about a
hapless puppet.

Pastels and gouache, 23" x 27"

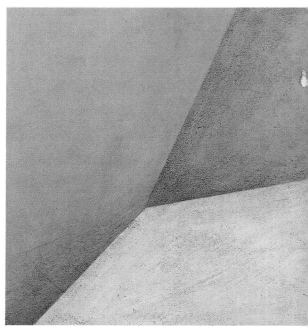

Illustrator: Marlene Hill Werner
Author: Jean Craighead George
Publisher: HarperCollins

Interior illustration from *The Moon of the Salamanders*,
which depicts the courtship ritual of the spotted
salamander.
Acrylic, 14″ x 21½″

Illustrator: Wallace E. Keller
Author: Wallace E. Keller
Publisher: Rizzoli International Publications

Cover and interior illustration from *The Wrong Side of
the Bed*, a tale of a boy who wakes up on the wrong side
of the bed and spends the rest of the day readjusting.
Acrylic and oil, 11″ x 36″

Illustrator: Cat Bowman Smith
Author: Marilyn Singer
Publisher: Henry Holt and Company

Interior illustration from *Chester, The Out-of-Work Dog*, the story of a farm dog's attempts to find a herding job after his family moves to town.
Ink and watercolor, 8" x 20"

Below
Illustrator: Allan Drummond
Author: Retold by Allan Drummond
Publisher: North-South Books

Interior illustration from *The Willow Pattern Story*, a retelling of the folktale based on the scene depicted on willow pattern china.
Gouache, crayon and pencil, 10½" x 26"

Illustrator: Beth Peck

Author: Paul Gallico

Publisher: Alfred A. Knopf

Interior illustration from *The Snow Goose*,
the story of a friendship between a young
girl and a hunchback, whose common bond
is the snow goose they both care for.

Oil, 22" x 16"

Illustrator: James Stevenson
Author: James Stevenson
Publisher: Greenwillow Books

Interior illustration from *Don't You Know There's a War On?*, in which the author recalls his childhood efforts to win World War II, including planting a victory garden, collecting tinfoil and looking for spies.
Watercolor, 20½" x 8½"

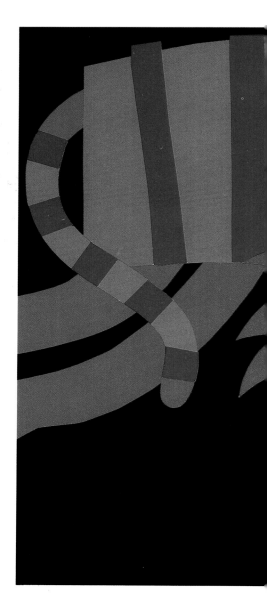

Illustrator: Jerry Pinkney
Author: Selected and edited by Colin Eisler
Publisher: Dial Books for Young Readers

Interior illustration from *David's Songs*, an illustrated interpretation of the Biblical psalms of David.
Pencil and watercolor, 11³/₄" x 19¹/₂"

Illustrator: Lois Ehlert
Author: Lois Ehlert
Publisher: HarperCollins

Interior illustration from *Circus*, a picture book about a circus performance.
Collage, 7¹/₄" x 12"

Illustrator: Anita Lobel

Author: Anita Lobel

Publisher: Western Publishing Co.

Interior illustration from *Pierrot's ABC Garden*, a picture book that teaches the alphabet as it tells the story of a clown picking vegetables and fruit from his garden.

Preseparated art in penline watercolor painted on nonphotographic blue boards, 10" x 12"

Right

Illustrator: Ted Lewin

Authors: Florence Parry Heide and Judith Heide Gilliland

Publisher: Clarion Books

Cover illustration from *Sami and the Time of the Troubles*, the story of a ten-year-old Lebanese boy who lives an ordinary life until bombings occur and fighting begins on his street.

Watercolor, 9¼" x 21"

Illustrator: Rosemary Wells

Author: Rosemary Wells

Publisher: Dial Books for Young Readers

Interior illustration from *Moss Pillows*, one of the three Voyage to the Bunny Planet books about a utopia headed by a bunny queen.

Watercolor and sepia ink, 5" x 5"

Illustrator: Gennady Spirin

Authors: Jakob and Wilhelm Grimm

Publisher: Philomel Books

Interior illustration from *Snow White & Rose Red*, the classic tale by the Brothers Grimm of a prince, turned into a bear by a wicked gnome, who is returned to his human form through the courage and kindness of two young girls.

Watercolor and pencil, 8¼" x 5⁹/₁₀"

Illustrator: Nancy Tafuri

Author: Mirra Ginsburg

Publisher: Greenwillow Books

Cover and interior illustration from *Asleep, Asleep*, a bedtime book that brings the reader into the heart of the night, when almost all the creatures of the earth are sleeping.

Watercolor ink, pastel and pen, 8¼" x 15¼"

Illustrator: Arthur Geisert

Author: Arthur Geisert

Publisher: Houghton Mifflin Co.

Promotional poster for *Oink*, whose design
includes all the book's illustrations.

Etching, 24" x 36"

Illustrator: Neil Waldman

Author: Nancy Luenn

Publisher: Atheneum Books for Children

Interior illustration from *Mother Earth*, an
illustrated ecological poem encouraging
readers to take care of the earth.

Watercolor, 10" x 16"

Right

Illustrator: Elise Primavera

Author: Diane Stanley

Publisher: G.P. Putnam's Sons

Interior illustration from *Moe the Dog in Tropical Paradise*, the story of how Moe and his friend Arlene create their own tropical paradise.

Watercolor, 13½" x 21"

Above

Illustrator: Daniel San Souci

Author: Retold by Margaret Hodges

Publisher: Charles Scribner's Sons Books for Young
Readers

Cover illustration from *The Golden Deer*, a retelling of an Indian folktale about how Buddha comes to earth in the form of a golden deer to protect a herd of deer from a king who hunts for pleasure.

Watercolor, 8" x 8"

Right

Illustrator: Aminah Brenda Lynn Robinson

Author: Michael J. Rosen

Publisher: Harcourt Brace Jovanovich

Interior illustration from *Elijah's Angel*, a story for Hanukkah and Christmas based on the life of Elijah Pierce, a barber and a renowned woodcarver.

House paint on scrap rag, 10" x 27"

Illustrator: Stefano Vitale
Author: Jim Aylesworth
Publisher: HarperCollins

Interior illustration from *The Folks in the Valley*, an alphabet book about the life of the Amish people.
Oil, 7" x 9"

Above

Illustrator: Stephen Gammell

Author: Jim Aylesworth

Publisher: Henry Holt and Company

Interior illustration from *Old Black Fly*, a picture book that teaches the alphabet as it recounts a day in the life of a housefly.

Crayon, oil pastel, colored pencil and watercolor, 13" x 10½"

Right

Illustrator: Suzanne Duranceau

Author: Robin Muller

Publisher: Scholastic Inc.

Interior illustration from *Hickory, Dickory, Dock*, a picture book that teaches how to tell time as it tells the story of animals on a treasure hunt.

Acrylic, 12½" x 12½"

Left

Illustrator: Barry Root

Author: Roberto Piumini

Publisher: Tambourine Books

Cover illustration from *The Saint and the Circus*, the story of a saint's attempt to help an acrobat, and the unforeseen consequences.

Watercolor and gouache, 11" x 8½"

Right

Illustrator: Paul Mirocha

Author: Jean Craighead George

Publisher: HarperCollins

Interior illustration from *The Moon of the Wild Pigs*, the story of a day in the life of a piglet that focuses on the many life-forms thriving in July in Arizona's Sonoron Desert.

Pastel and colored pencil, 12" x 9"

Right

Illustrator: Heidi Goennel

Author: Heidi Goennel

Publisher: Tambourine Books

Interior illustration from *The Circus*, a picture book about going to the circus.

Acrylic, 11½" x 17½"

Illustrator: Peter Sis

Author: Peter Sis

Publisher: Greenwillow Books

Cover and interior illustration from *An Ocean World*, the story of a young whale, born and raised in captivity, who experiences the ocean for the first time.

Watercolor, 12" x 15"

Illustrator: Pat Cummings

Author: Pat Cummings

Publisher: Bradbury Press

Interior illustration from *Petey Moroni's Camp Runamok Diary*, a camper's chronicle of the rapid disappearance of food as an unseen raccoon eludes campers for two weeks.

Gouache, 10" x 18"

Left
Illustrator: Michael Garland
Author: Washington Irving (1783-1859)
Publisher: Boyds Mills Press

Cover illustration from *The Legend of Sleepy Hollow*, an illustrated version of Washington Irving's classic tale.
Oil, 14" x 11"

Below
Illustrator: Ed Young
Author: Mary Calhoun
Publisher: Morrow Junior Books

Interior illustration from *While I Sleep*, a parent-child dialogue on various animals and things that take rest in the course of a night.
Pastel, 11" x 17"

Illustrator: Jerry Pinkney

Author: Gloria Jean Pinkney

Publisher: Dial Books for Young Readers

Interior illustration from *Back Home*, a celebration of an African-American child's discovery of her family's rural roots.

Pencil and watercolor, 10¾" x 17½"

Illustrator: Maryjane Begin
Author: Diane Wolkstein
Publisher: Morrow Junior Books

Interior illustration from *Little Mouse's Painting*, a story about a painting misunderstood by the artist's friends.
Watercolor and acrylic, 8³/₄" x 8¹/₄"

Illustrator: Donald Crews
Author: Donald Crews
Publisher: Greenwillow Books

Interior illustration from *Shortcut*, a story, based on an event in the author's life, of a group of children who take a shortcut along the rail line, and the consequences of their shortcut.
Watercolor and gouache, 8¹/₄" x 20"

Above

Illustrator: Patricia Polacco

Author: Patricia Polacco

Publisher: Philomel Books

Interior illustration from *Chicken Sunday*, the story of two African-American boys and a Russian girl who are blamed for vandalizing a shop, and the lesson they learn.

Pentel markers, acrylic, pencil and pastels, 15" x 22"

Above

Illustrator: Floyd Cooper

Author: Retold by Jean Merrill

Publisher: Philomel Books

Cover illustration from *The Girl Who Loved Caterpillars*, an adaptation of an anonymous twelfth-century Japanese story about a young woman whose independence resists social and family pressures.

Oil wash on board, 14½" x 24"

Right

Illustrator: M. Lisa Etre

Author: S.T. Garne

Publisher: Simon & Schuster/Green Tiger Press

Interior illustration from *One White Sail*, a children's counting book influenced by West Indian culture.

Gouache, 9" x 9"

Right

Illustrator: Stephen Marchesi

Author: Adapted by Margaret Hodges

Publisher: Charles Scribner's Sons Books for
    Young Readers

Interior illustration from *Don Quixote and
Sancho Panza*, a retelling of Cervantes'
classic seventeenth-century novel.

Oil, alkyd and pencil, 12" x 10"

Below

Illustrator: Michael Paraskevas

Author: Betty Paraskevas

Publisher: Dial Books for Young Readers

Interior illustration from *On the Edge of the Sea*, the
story of a boy who dreams that he lives on the edge of
the sea in a castle of sand.

Acrylic, 31" x 52"

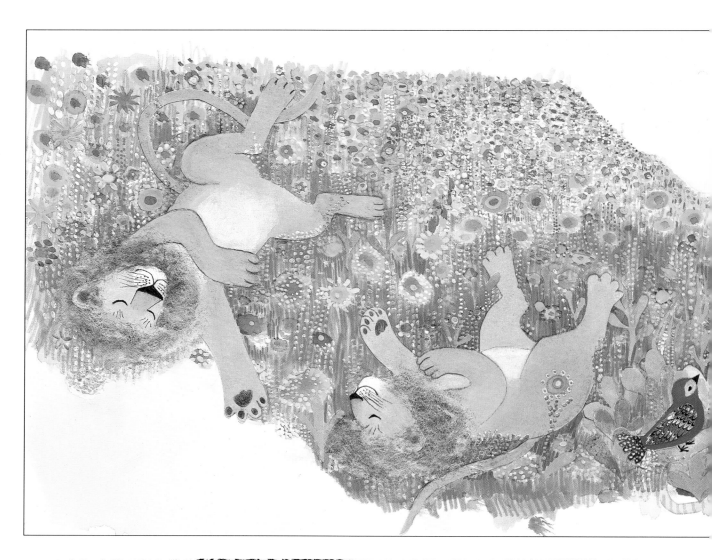

Illustrator: Elisa Kleven

Author: Elisa Kleven

Publisher: E.P. Dutton Children's Books

Interior illustration from *The Lion and the Little Red Bird*, the story of the friendship between a lion and a bird.

Collage, watercolor, pastel, ink, cut paper and lambswool, 8" x 18½"

Illustrator: Ashley Bryan

Author: Ashley Bryan

Publisher: HarperCollins

Cover and interior illustration from *Sing to the Sun*, an illustrated book of poems celebrating life in the Caribbean.

Watercolor, 6½" x 5"

Left

Illustrator: Brian Pinkney

Author: Robert D. San Souci

Publisher: Four Winds Press

Interior illustration from *Sukey and the Mermaid*, an adaptation of an African-American folktale about a little girl's friendship with a mermaid.

Oil pastels on scratchboard, 10" x 18½"

Top

Illustrator: Grayce Bochak

Author: Rabindranath Tagore (1861-1941)

Publisher: Boyds Mills Press

Cover illustration from *Paper Boats*, a poem by the Indian writer and Nobel Prize winner about a young boy in India.

Cut paper on acid-free foamboard, 10" x 22½"

Above

Illustrator: Gennady Spirin

Author: Claire Martin

Publisher: Dial Books for Young Readers

Interior illustration from *Boots & the Glass Mountain,* an adaptation of the Brothers Grimm tale.

Watercolor, 8¾" x 15"

Above

Illustrator: Robert Quackenbush

Author: Robert Quackenbush

Publisher: Pippin Press

Cover illustration from *Lost in the Amazon*, a mystery set in the Amazon rain forest and starring "ducktective" Miss Mallard. Watercolor, 9¹/₂″ x 15¹/₂″

Right

Illustrator: Betsy Lewin

Author: Russell Hoban

Publisher: Clarion Books

Interior illustration from *Jim Hedgehog and the Lonesome Tower*, the story of a heavy metal fan whose purchase of a new cassette leads him into an adventure. Fiber-tip pen and watercolor, 8″ x 11″

Illustrator: Michael McCurdy
Author: X.J. Kennedy
Publisher: Macmillan

Interior illustration from *The Beasts of Bethlehem*, a book of nineteen poems about animals that could have been present at the Nativity.
Scratchboard and colored pencils, 6½" x 4"

Illustrator: Gerald McDermott
Author: Gerald McDermott
Publisher: Harcourt Brace Jovanovich

Interior illustration from *Zomo the Rabbit*, a tale, based on West African folklore, about a trickster rabbit and his quest for wisdom.
Gouache, 10" x 24"

Illustrator: Petra Mathers
Author: Richard Kennedy
Publisher: Alfred A. Knopf

Interior illustration from *Little Love Song*, the tale of a woman small enough to live in a peanut shell, and the man who falls in love with her.
Watercolor, 6" x 6"

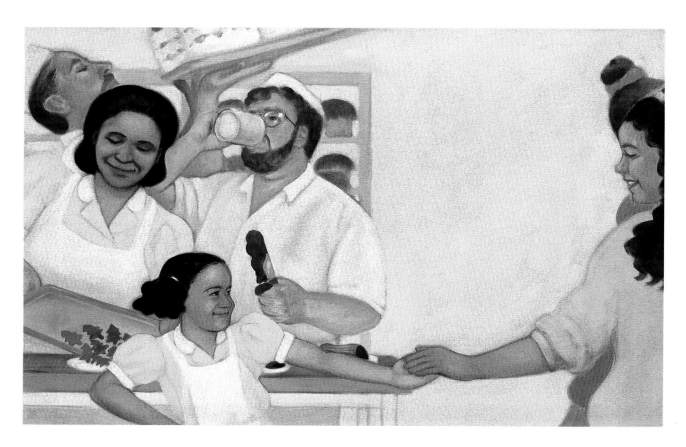

Above

Illustrator: Sheila Hamanaka

Author: Amy Heath

Publisher: Four Winds Press

Interior illustration from *Sofie's Role*, the story of a little girl who helps at her family's bakery at Christmastime.

Oil, 22" x 34"

Right

Illustrator: Dale Gottlieb

Author: Dale Gottlieb

Publisher: Alfred A. Knopf

Cover and interior illustration from *Seeing Eye Willie*, the tale of a little girl and the story she makes up about a homeless man she often sees.

Oil crayon on rag paper, 19¼" x 19¼"

Above

Illustrator: John O'Brien
Author: Edward Lear
Publisher: Boyds Mills Press

Interior illustration from *Daffy Down Dillies*,
an illustrated collection of limericks by
Edward Lear.
Pen and ink, watercolor and dyes, 11" x 17"

Illustrator: Glenn Halak
Author: Glenn Halak
Publisher: Green Tiger Press

Interior illustration from *A Grandmother's Story*, the tale
of a grandmother and how she saves her grandson's life.
Watercolor, 10½" x 14"

Below

Illustrator: Lindsay Barrett George

Author: William T. George

Publisher: Greenwillow Books

Interior illustration from *Christmas at Long Pond*, the story of a father and son who observe the plant and animal life around Long Pond before choosing a Christmas tree.

Gouache, 13" x 21"

Left

Illustrator: Chris Conover

Author: Chris Conover

Publisher: Farrar, Straus and Giroux

Interior illustration from *Sam Panda and Thunder Dragon*, the story of the unlikely friendship between a panda and a dragon, and its fortuitous results.

Watercolor and pen and ink, 11" x 9"

Below

Illustrator: Eve Chwast

Author: Malka Drucker

Publisher: Harcourt Brace Jovanovich

Cover and interior illustration from *Grandma's Latkes,* wherein Grandma and Molly make latkes while Grandma tells Molly the history of Hanukkah.

Woodcuts painted with watercolor, 10" x 11"

Illustrator: Johanna Westerman

Author: Retold by Valerie Scho Carey

Publisher: Arcade Publishing

Cover and interior illustration from *Maggie Mab and the Bogey Beast,* an adaptation of a traditional English fairy tale about an optimistic old woman's run-in with the fabled bogey beast.

Watercolor, 10" x 7"

Below

Illustrator: Thacher Hurd

Author: Thacher Hurd

Publisher: Crown Books for Young Readers

Interior illustration from *Tomato Soup*, a picture book describing an incident between a cat and a mouse on a farm.

Watercolor, 11" x 17"

Illustrator: Richard Hull

Author: Jim Aylesworth

Publisher: Atheneum Books for Children

Cover and interior illustration from *The Cat & The Fiddle & More*, a book that plays off the song "Hey Diddle Diddle" and comes up with some fanciful alternative rhymes.

Colored pencil over oil wash, 10½" x 16½"

Illustrator: Catherine Stock

Author: Lynn Joseph

Publisher: Clarion Books

Cover and interior illustration from *An Island Christmas*,
the story of a girl in Trinidad, and what she does to
prepare for Christmas.

Watercolor, 10" x 16"

Above
Illustrator: Carole Byard
Author: Sherley Anne Williams
Publisher: Harcourt Brace Jovanovich

Interior illustration from *Working Cotton*, about a little girl's day in the cotton fields with her family.
Acrylic, 20" x 35½"

Left
Illustrator: Maggie Smith
Author: Maggie Smith
Publisher: Lothrop, Lee & Shepard

Interior illustration from *My Grandma's Chair*, the story of the adventures a child imagines in his grandmother's chair.
Mixed media, 8¼" x 16½"

Left

Illustrator: S.D. Schindler

Author: Megan McDonald

Publisher: Orchard Books

Cover illustration from *Whoo-oo Is It?*, the tale of a mother owl who hears various sounds in the night and finally realizes they're coming from her unhatched chicks. Pastel, 9³/₄" x 9¹/₂"

Below

Illustrator: Dominic Catalano

Author: Dominic Catalano

Publisher: Philomel Books

Cover illustration from *Wolf Plays Alone*, the story of a wolf who deals with constant interruptions as he tries to play his trumpet. Carbon pencil, airbrushed watercolor, and colored pencil, 11¹/₂" x 17³/₄"

Illustrator: Anita Lobel

Author: Charlotte Zolotow

Publisher: Greenwillow Books

Interior illustration from *This Quiet Lady*, a
book wherein a little girl looks at her
mother's life in pictures.

Gouache, 9³/₄″ x 8¹/₂″

Above

Illustrator: Friso Henstra

Author: Elsa Marston

Publisher: Tambourine Books

Cover and interior illustration from *Cynthia and the Runaway Gazebo,* the tale of a young girl at a garden party who is suddenly swept out to sea with her friends in a white gazebo.

Watercolor and ink, 12½" x 20½"

Illustrator: Paul Rátz de Tagyos

Author: Paul Rátz de Tagyos

Publisher: Clarion Books

Interior illustration from *A Coney Tale,* the story of a village of rabbits in seventeenth-century Flanders.

Marker, pencil, ink and pastel on rag marker paper, 7" x 18"

Left

Illustrator: Dale Gottlieb

Author: Eve Merriam

Publisher: Henry Holt and Company

Interior illustration from *Train Leaves the Station*, in which a toy train and its occupants make a journey that introduces the numbers one to ten.

Gouache, 11" x 8½"

Illustrator: Oscar de Mejo

Author: Oscar de Mejo

Publisher: HarperCollins

Interior illustration from *Oscar de Mejo's ABC*, a series of
paintings that illustrate scenes from Americana for each
letter of the alphabet.

Acrylic, 22" x 18"

Above

Illustrator: James Endicott

Author: Harry Behn

Publisher: Henry Holt and Company

Interior illustration from *Trees*, an illustrated poem about the subject.

Watercolor, 12" x 18"

Right

Illustrator: Stephen T. Johnson

Author: Retold by Melissa Hayden

Publisher: Andrews and McMeel

Cover and interior illustration from *The Nutcracker Ballet*, an interpretation of the classic ballet in which a Victorian girl travels from her parlor to the land of sweets.

Pastel and watercolor, 21" x 16¼"

Above

Illustrator: Barry Root

Author: Mary Lyn Ray

Publisher: Harcourt Brace
    Jovanovich

Interior illustration from
Pumpkins, the story of a man
and a field who collaborate
to save the field from
development.

Watercolor and gouache, 12" x 26"

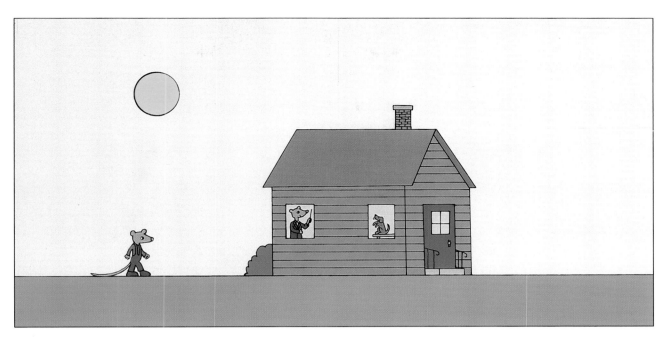

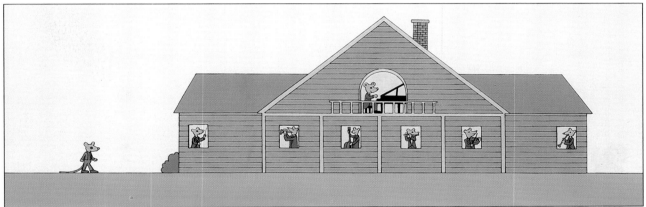

Illustrator: Frank Asch

Author: Frank Asch

Publisher: Scholastic Inc.

Interior illustration from *Little Fish, Big Fish*, a fold-out book exploring the concept of opposites. At top: "little house"; at bottom: "big house."

Acrylic, 8" x 16"

Left

Illustrator: Jonathan Green

Author: Denizé Lauture

Publisher: Philomel Books

Cover and interior illustration from *Father and Son*, a picture book about the bonding between a boy and his father.

Oil, 14" x 11"

Above

Illustrator: Arden Johnson

Author: Jan Wahl

Publisher: Tambourine Books

Interior illustration from *The Sleepytime Book,* an illustrated lullaby verse telling how various creatures settle in for the night.

Pastel, 20″ x 30″

Right

Illustrator: Lizi Boyd

Author: Lizi Boyd

Publisher: Viking

Cover and interior illustration from *Sweet Dreams, Willy*, the story of a boy who, reluctant to go to bed, goes off in search of others who are still awake.

Gouache, 5″ x 16½″

Illustrator: Lloyd Bloom

Author: Gloria Houston

Publisher: Philomel Books

Interior illustration from *But No Candy*, the story of a little girl growing up during World War II.

Acrylic, 14¼" x 11⅜"

Illustrator: Brad Sneed
Author: Brad Sneed
Publisher: G.P. Putnam's Sons

Interior illustration from *Lucky Russell,* the tale of Russell the kitten and his search for something to do on his farm.
Watercolor, 11⅝" x 9¼"

Below
Illustrator: Roger Roth
Author: Nancy Milton
Publisher: Crown Publishers, Inc.

Interior illustration from *The Giraffe That Walked to Paris*, the true story of the first giraffe to come to France.
Watercolor and pencil, 9½" x 20½"

Illustrator: Henrik Drescher

Author: Eric Metaxas

Publisher: Rabbit Ears Books/Picture Book Studio

Cover and interior illustration from *The Fool and the Flying Ship*, an adaptation of a Russian folktale about a bumpkin's quest to win the hand of the Tsar's daughter.

Watercolor and ink, 16" x 17"

Illustrator: Sue Truesdell
Author: Laura Geringer
Publisher: HarperCollins

Interior illustration from *Look Out, Look Out, It's Coming!*, the story of a huge creature who follows a boy home and bounds through his window during dinner, changing his family's life in chaotic and humorous ways.
Ink and watercolor, 8" x 20"

Illustrator: Ted Lewin
Author: Megan McDonald
Publisher: Orchard Books

Interior illustration from *The Great Pumpkin Switch*, the story of a pair of boys who replace a squashed pumpkin, with fortuitous results.
Watercolor, 9" x 20"

Below

Illustrator: Dorothée Duntze

Author: Dorothée Duntze

Publisher: North-South Books

Interior illustration from *The Twelve Days of Christmas*, an illustrated version of the classic Christmas carol.

Acrylics, ink, white gouache and colored pencil, 11" x 17"

Illustrator: Stephen T. Johnson

Author: Retold by Robert D. San Souci

Publisher: Dial Books for Young Readers

Cover and interior illustration from *The Samurai's Daughter,* a retelling of a
Japanese folktale about the brave daughter of a Samurai warrior and her journey
to be reunited with her exiled father.

Pastel and watercolor, 16¼" x 14⅜"

Illustrator: Christopher Manson
Author: Christopher Manson
Publisher: North-South Books

Interior illustration from *A Farmyard Song,* a rhyming picture book in which various farm animals make appropriate noises after being fed.
Woodcuts and watercolors, 9½" x 10½"

Below
Illustrator: Vivienne Flesher
Author: Retold by D.J. MacHale
Publisher: Rabbit Ears Books/Picture Book Studio

Interior illustration from *East of the Sun, West of the Moon,* a picture book retelling the classic folktale of a girl's quest to free her beloved prince from a magic spell.
Pastel, 24" x 36"

Above left

Illustrator: Sheila Hamanaka

Author: Marguerite W. Davol

Publisher: Simon & Schuster

Illustration from *The Heart of the Wood*, a description of how a tree is felled, milled and turned into a violin.

Oil on bark paper, 15" x 23"

Left

Illustrator: Alexi Natchev

Author: Becky Hickox Ayres

Publisher: Doubleday Books for Young Readers

Cover and interior illustration from *Matreshka*, a story, inspired by Russian folklore, about a magic wooden doll that rescues its kidnapped young owner.

Watercolor and colored pencil, 12" x 18"

Above

Illustrator: Robert Quackenbush

Author: Robert Quackenbush

Publisher: Pippin Press

Cover illustration from *Evil Under the Sea*, a mystery set in Australia and starring "ducktective" Miss Mallard.

Watercolor, 9½" x 15½"

Above

Illustrator: Lynn Munsinger

Author: Selected by William Cole

Publisher: Houghton Mifflin Co.

Interior illustration from *A Zooful of Animals,* a collection of humorous poems about animals.

Watercolor and ink, 11½" x 18"

Illustrator: Wil Clay

Author: Margaret Sacks

Publisher: Lodestar Books

Cover illustration from *Themba,* a book about a South African boy's search for his father.

Acrylic, 18½" x 25½"

Above

Illustrator: Jerry Pinkney
Author: Virginia Hamilton
Publisher: Harcourt Brace Jovanovich

Interior illustration from *Drylongso,* a picture book that tells the story of the struggle of a farm family to survive a drought.

Pencil, watercolor and pastel, 12¼" x 19½"

Left

Illustrator: William Noonan
Author: Paul Robert Walker
Publisher: Harcourt Brace Jovanovich

Cover and interior illustration from *Bigfoot and Other Legendary Creatures,* a blend of fiction and nonfiction about seven mythical creatures.

Watercolor, 18" x 10"

The Very Best of Children's Book Illustration   101

Illustrator: Carla Golembe

Author: Retold by Mary Joan Gerson

Publisher: Joy Street Books/Little, Brown & Co.

Interior illustration from *Why the Sky Is Far Away,* an adaptation of a 400-year-old Nigerian pourquoi tale with an ecological message.

Monotype with oil pastel, 27" x 30"

Illustrator: David DeRan
Author: Linda Lowe Morris
Publisher: Rabbit Ears Books/Picture Book Studio

Cover and interior illustration from *Morning Milking,* a picture book about a child who helps her father milk cows one winter morning.
Watercolor, 13" x 9"

Illustrator: Charles Mikolaycak
Author: Retold by Charles Mikolaycak
Publisher: Harcourt Brace Jovanovich

Cover and interior illustration from *Orpheus,* a retelling of the Greek myth of the musician Orpheus and his wife Euridyce.
Colored pencil, watercolor and acrylic, 7¼" x 15"

Above

Illustrator: David Soman

Author: Angela Johnson

Publisher: Orchard Books

Interior illustration from *The Leaving Morning,* the story of a family packing and saying goodbye to their neighborhood as they prepare to move.

Watercolor, 14½" x 24½"

Illustrator: Mary Barrett Brown

Author: Mary Barrett Brown

Publisher: Orchard Books

Cover and interior illustration from *Wings Along the Waterway*, a book about the appearance and habits of birds seen along waterways.

Watercolor, 11" x 17"

Illustrator: Ted Lewin

Author: Frances Ward Weller

Publisher: Macmillan Publishing Company

Interior illustration from *Matthew Wheelock's Wall,* a picture book about a wall that a farmer builds to last 100 years.

Watercolor, 8" x 20"

"Well, maybe we've got to go home now," said the dragons.

"Wait!" yelled the nurse. "Come back!"

Above left

Illustrator: Brian Pinkney

Author: Judy Sierra

Publisher: Lodestar Books

Interior illustration from *The Elephant's Wrestling Match*, an adaptation of an African folktale about a mighty elephant bested by a tiny bat in a battle of wits.

Oil on scratchboard, 10½" x 16"

Left

Illustrator: Michael J. Woods

Author: Felix Salten

Publisher: Simon & Schuster Books for
    Young Readers

Interior illustration from *Bambi*, a new edition of the classic story of a young deer's life.

Watercolor, 11" x 18"

Above

Illustrator: Janet Street

Author: Lynne Bertrand

Publisher: Clarkson Potter

Interior illustration from *One Day, Two Dragons*, the tale of two dragons' trip to the doctor.

Watercolor, 7½" x 9½"

Above

Illustrator: Michael Grejniec

Author: Michael Grejniec

Publisher: North-South Books

Interior illustration from *What Do You Like?*, a picture book designed to stimulate a child's imagination.
Watercolor, 5" x 8"

Right

Illustrator: Rosemary Wells

Author: Rosemary Wells

Publisher: Dial Books for Young Readers

Interior illustration from *First Tomato,* one of the three Voyage to the Bunny Planet books about a utopia headed by a bunny queen.
Watercolor and sepia ink, 5" x 5"

Illustrator: Cathi Hepworth

Author: Cathi Hepworth

Publisher: G.P. Putnam's Sons

Interior illustration from *Antics!*, a run through the alphabet wherein each word contains the word "ant." Shown above: "tantrum."

Pastel and colored pencil, 6⅝" x 5¼"

Above
Illustrator: Steve Johnson
Author: Marsha Wilson Chall
Publisher: Lothrop, Lee & Shepard

Interior illustration from *Up North at the Cabin,* a picture book describing a girl's summer vacation up north at the cabin, and her memorable experiences with nature that summer.
Acrylic, 12¹/₅" x 20¹/₂"

Illustrator: Normand Chartier
Author: Ellen Jackson
Publisher: Macmillan Children's Books

Interior illustration from *Boris the Boring Boar,* the tale of a boring boar whose encounter with a wolf teaches him the value of being a good listener.
Pencil and watercolor, 10" x 8"

Top

Illustrator: Susan Gaber

Author: Jacqueline Briggs Martin

Publisher: HarperCollins

Interior illustration from *The Finest Horse in Town,* a story, set at the turn of the century in Maine, about a horse that became legendary in its owners' family.

Watercolor and colored pencil, 6¼" x 11¼"

Above

Illustrator: Michael McCurdy

Author: Michael McCurdy

Publisher: G.P. Putnam's Sons

Interior illustration from *The Old Man and the Fiddle,* the story of a stubborn old man who won't stop playing his fiddle.

Woodcuts, 9" x 15"

Illustrator: Mark Buehner
Authors: Caralyn and Mark Buehner
Publisher: Dial Books for Young Readers

Cover and interior illustration from *The Escape of Marvin the Ape,* a story about an ape who escapes from the zoo and experiences the excitement of city life.

Oil over acrylic, 13³⁄₄″ x 15³⁄₄″

Illustrator: John Sandford
Author: Phyllis Root
Publisher: Arcade Publishing

Interior illustration from *The Old Red Rocking Chair,* the tale of a rocking chair and how it makes its way from neighbor to neighbor and how it finally ends up back in the original owner's possession.

Oil, 16″ x 20″

Left
Illustrator: Betsy Lewin
Author: Grace Maccarone
Publisher: Scholastic Inc.

Interior illustration from *Itchy, Itchy Chicken Pox,* the story of how a boy copes with the common childhood illness.
Fiber-tip pen and watercolor, 9" x 6"

Below
Illustrator: Diane deGroat
Author: Carol P. Saul
Publisher: Simon & Schuster Books for Young Readers

Interior illustration from *Peter's Song,* the tale of a pig with a song who finds a frog who appreciates it.
Watercolor, Prismacolor and acrylic, 10" x 16"

Left

Illustrator: Andrew Shachat

Author: Tedd Arnold

Publisher: Dial Books for Young Readers

Cover illustration from *The Simple People,* a tale with an environmental message about how people alter their surroundings.

Watercolor, acrylic, colored inks and varnish, 10⅜″ x 8¾″

Right

Illustrator: Oki S. Han

Author: Adapted by Oki S. Han and
        Stephanie Haboush Plunkett

Publisher: Dial Books for Young Readers

Cover and interior illustration from *Sir Whong and the Golden Pig,* the story of a stranger who tries to outwit the wise and generous Sir Whong by giving a fake golden pig as collateral for his loan.

Watercolor, 8½″ x 11″

Illustrator: Olivier Dunrea

Author: Olivier Dunrea

Publisher: Doubleday

Interior illustration from *The Broody Hen,* a picture book about a hen on a medieval European farm.

Watercolor, 9″ x 9 ¾″

Illustrator: Shari Halpern

Author: Shari Halpern

Publisher: Macmillan Children's Books

Interior illustration from *My River,* a book depicting a
variety of river animals.

Collage with painted and cut paper, 8¼" x 15¾"

Illustrator: David Wiesner
Author: David Wiesner
Publisher: Clarion Books

Interior illustration from *June 29, 1999,* the story of a third-grade science experiment which goes awry, and the gigantic vegetables from space that may or may not have been the result.
Watercolor, 10" x 20½"

Below
Illustrator: Demi
Author: Selected by Demi, translated by
    Tze-si Huang
Publisher: Henry Holt and Company

Cover and interior illustration from *In the Eyes of the Cat,* a collection of Japanese nature poems organized according to seasons.
Watercolor, 5½" x 7½"

Below

Illustrator: Patricia Polacco

Author: Patricia Polacco

Publisher: Bantam Books

Cover and interior illustration from *Mrs. Katz and Tush,* the story of an elderly Polish woman and an African-American boy who discover their commonalities.

Pentel markers, acrylic, pencil and pastels, 15" x 22"

Above

Illustrator: Kurt Vargö

Author: Brian Gleeson

Publisher: Rabbit Ears Books/Picture Book
    Studio

Interior illustration from *The Tiger and the Brahmin,* the tale of a holy man who is deceived by a hungry tiger and who is saved by the cleverness of a jackal.

Pastel and oil, 7½" x 9½"

Above right

Illustrator: Edward Sorel

Author: Eric Metaxas

Publisher: Rabbit Ears Books/Picture Book
    Studio

Cover illustration from *Jack and the Beanstalk,* a retelling of the classic folktale.

Pen, ink and watercolor, 14" x 17"

Right

Illustrator: Janet Street

Author: Allen L. Sirois

Publisher: Tambourine Books

Interior illustration from *Dinosaur Dress Up,* a cautionary tale in which Professor Saurus guides the reader through the world of fossil fashions.

Watercolor, 8¼" x 17"

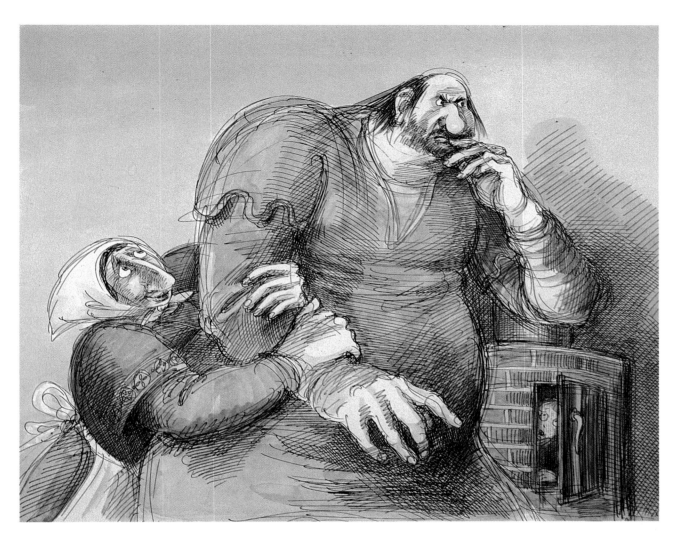

Illustrator: Barry Moser

Author: George Frideric Handel (1685-1759)

Publisher: HarperCollins

Interior illustration from *Messiah,* an illustrated edition
of the libretto for Handel's popular choral work.

Watercolor on handmade paper, 7½" x 6"

Illustrator: Melanie Hope Greenberg

Author: Kathleen Krull

Publisher: Doubleday

Cover and interior illustration from *It's My Earth, Too,* an ecology book for the very young produced in an environmentally friendly manner.

Gouache, pen and pencils, 7¹/₂" x 7¹/₂"

Below

Illustrator: Robert J. Blake

Author: Ann Turner

Publisher: HarperCollins

Interior illustration from *Rainflowers,* a picture book about the reactions of a farm's inhabitants to a thunderstorm.

Watercolor, 13¹/₂" x 20"

Left

Illustrator: Samuel Byrd

Author: Myra Cohn Livingston

Publisher: Holiday House

Cover illustration from *Let Freedom Ring: A Ballad of Martin Luther King, Jr.,* a biography for children of the slain civil rights leader.

Watercolor and colored pencil, 12" x 8½"

Right

Illustrator: Simms Taback

Authors: Katy Hall and Lisa Eisenberg

Publisher: Dial Books for Young Readers

Interior illustration from *Spacey Riddles,* an illustrated book of riddles for younger readers.

India ink, watercolor and colored pencil, 7⅛" x 4½"

Below

Illustrator: Juan Wijngaard

Author: Wendy Cheyette Lewison

Publisher: Dial Books for Young Readers

Interior illustration from *Going to Sleep on the Farm,* a father and son's conversation about farm animals and their sleeping habits.

Watercolor, 8¼" x 15"

Above

Illustrator: Elaine Greenstein

Author: Elaine Greenstein

Publisher: Picture Book Studio

Cover illustration from *Emily and the Crows,* the story of a girl who pretends to be a crow to find out why Emily the cow is popular with crows.

Casein paint and ink, 6¼" x 8¾"

Illustrator: Lois Ehlert

Author: Adaptation of Peruvian folktale, translated into Spanish by Amy Prince

Publisher: Harcourt Brace Jovanovich

Interior illustration from *Moon Rope (Un lazo a la luna),* a retelling of a Peruvian folktale, with art inspired by pre-Columbian artifacts, and with a Spanish-English text.

Collage and silver ink, 12" x 10"

Illustrator: N. Cameron Watson
Author: Clyde Watson
Publisher: Macmillan Publishing Company

Interior illustration from *Mister Toad*, the tale of a toad whose peaceful lifestyle is threatened by inconsiderate neighbors, and how he deals with them.
Watercolor, 5½" x 5½"

Below
Illustrator: Mark Alan Weatherby
Author: Jim Murphy
Publisher: Scholastic Inc.

Cover and interior illustration from *Dinosaur for a Day,* the story of a day in a dinosaur's life.
Acrylic, 15" x 23⅝"

Above left

Illustrator: Ted Rand

Author: Charles E. Carryl (1841-1920)

Publisher: Arcade Publishing

Interior illustration from *The Walloping Window-Blind,* an illustrated version of a classic nonsense poem.

Chalk, watercolor and Prismacolor, 13¼" x 22½"

Left

Illustrator: Debra Frasier

Author: William Stafford

Publisher: Harcourt Brace Jovanovich

Cover and interior illustration from *The Animal That Drank Up Sound,* an interpretation of William Stafford's metaphorical poem about a cricket who braves the silence of winter to restore sound, and spring, to the world.

Collage, 14" x 32¼"

Above

Illustrator: Jeanette Winter

Author: Jeanette Winter

Publisher: Alfred A. Knopf

Interior illustration from *Klara's New World,* the tale of a Swedish family who immigrates to America in the 1800s.

Acrylic, 8⅛" x 9⅛"

Above

Illustrator: Kathryn Brown

Author: Jane Yolen

Publisher: Harcourt Brace Jovanovich

Cover and interior illustration from *Eeny, Meeny, Miney Mole*, the story of a mole who goes against the advice of her cynical sisters and befriends neighboring creatures, who lead her to discover the world above.

Watercolor, 7" x 9"

Right

Illustrator: Oscar de Mejo

Author: Oscar de Mejo

Publisher: Philomel Books

Interior illustration from *The Professor of Etiquette*, a guide to the dos and don'ts of civilized living.

Watercolor and graphite, 7" x 6"

Above

Illustrator: Simon Henwood

Author: Simon Henwood

Publisher: Farrar Straus & Giroux

Interior illustration from *The Hidden Jungle,* the tale of an introspective hero's efforts to relocate a dying tree.
Gouache, 18" x 27"

Left

Illustrator: Kimberly Bulcken Root

Author: Jennifer Armstrong

Publisher: Crown Books for Young Readers

Cover and interior illustration from *Hugh Can Do,* the tale of a boy whose good deeds are repaid to him.
Pen and ink and watercolor, 11" x 8½"

Credits and Permissions

The following pieces are used by permission of the copyright owner.

Page 6, "Northern Lights Dance," illustration from *Northern Lullaby* © 1992 Leo and Diane Dillon. Art Director: Nanette Stevenson.

Page 7, illustration from *The Orange Book* by Richard McGuire, © Rizzoli International Publications. Art Director: Richard McGuire and Susan Carpenter.

Page 7, illustration from *Bently & egg* © 1992 William Joyce. Art Director: Christine Kettner.

Page 8, reprinted with permission of Atheneum Publishers, an imprint of Macmillan Publishing Company from *And in the Beginning...* by Sheron Williams, illustrated by Robert Roth. Illustrations © 1992 Robert Roth. Art Director: Patrice Fodero.

Page 8, illustration from *The Island Light* © Rosemary Wells. Art Director: Atha Tehon.

Page 9, illustration from *Boots and His Brothers* © Kimberly Bulcken Root. Art Director: Tere LoPrete.

Page 10, illustration from *Six Creepy Sheep* © 1992 John O'Brien. Art Director: Tim Gillner.

Page 10-11, illustration from *The Fortune-Tellers* © 1992 Trina Schart Hyman. Art Director: Riki Levinson.

Page 11, "Feathertop," illustration from *Feathertop* © 1992 Daniel San Souci. Art Director: Lynn Braswell.

Page 12, illustration from *Bootsie Barker Bites* © 1992 Peggy Rathmann. Art Director: Nanette Stevenson.

Page 12, illustration from *Charlie Parker Played Be Bop* © 1992 Christopher Raschka. Art Director: Mina Greenstein.

Page 13, cover illustration from *The Seashore Book* © Wendell Minor. Art Directors: Wendell Minor and Al Cetta.

Page 14, illustration from *Count!* © 1992 Denise Fleming. Art Director: Maryann Leffingwell.

Page 14, illustration from *The Antique Store Cat* © Leslie Baker. Art Director: Susan Lu.

Page 15, illustration from *Busy Buzzing Bumblebees* © 1992 Paul Meisel. Art Director: Christine Kettner.

Page 16, illustration from *One Yellow Lion* © 1992 Matthew Van Fleet. Art Director: Atha Tehon.

Page 16-17, illustration from *If You Ever Meet a Whale* © 1992 Leonard Everett Fisher. Art Director: Tere LoPrete.

Page 17, "Seven Conch Shells," illustration from *One Smiling Grandma* © 1992 Lynne Russell, first published in Great Britain by Heinemann Young Books. Art Director: Atha Tehon.

Page 18, illustration from *Matthew's Meadow* © Ted Lewin. Art Director: Michael Farmer. Designer: Camilla Filancia.

Page 18-19, illustration from *Where the Buffalo Roam* © 1992 Jacqueline A. Geis. Art Director: Joy Chu.

Page 19, illustration from *Flyaway Girl* © 1992 Ann Grifalconi. Art Director: Susan Lu.

Page 20, illustration by Frané Lessac from *Caribbean Carnival* by Irving Burgie. Illustrations © 1992 Frané Lessac. Reprinted by permission of Tambourine Books, a division of William Morrow & Company, Inc. Art Director: Golda Laurens.

Page 21, illustration by Jim LaMarche from *The Rainbabies* by Laura Krauss Melmed. Illustrations © 1992 Jim LaMarche. Reprinted by permission of Lothrop, Lee & Shepard Books, a division of William Morrow & Company, Inc. Art Director: Rachel Pearson.

Page 21, illustration by Douglas Florian from his *At the Zoo* © 1992 Douglas Florian. Reprinted by permission of Greenwillow Books, a division of William Morrow & Company, Inc. Art Director: Ava Weiss.

Page 22, illustration from *The Rough-Face Girl* © 1992 David Shannon. Art Directors: Gunta Alexander and Nanette Stevenson.

Page 22, illustration from *Ma'ii and Cousin Horned Toad* © Shonto Begay. Art Director: Claire B. Counihan.

Page 23, illustration from *Kenji and the Magic Geese* © Jean and Mou-Sien Tseng. Art Director: Lucille Chomowicz.

Page 24, illustration from *Aunt Elaine Does the Dance from Spain* © Petra Mathers. Art Director: Lynn Braswell.

Page 24, illustration from *A Ride on the Red Mare's Back* © 1992 Julie Downing. Art Director: Mina Greenstein.

Page 25, "Don't Be Sad, Sweet Girl," illustration from *Waiting for the Whales* © 1991 Ron Lightburn. Art Director: Ron Lightburn. Designers: Christine Toller and Ron Lightburn.

Page 26, illustration by John O'Brien from *Brother Billy Bronto's Bygone Blues Band* by David F. Birchman. Illustrations © 1992 John O'Brien. Reprinted by permission of Lothrop, Lee & Shepard Books, a division of William Morrow & Company, Inc. Art Director: Rachel Simon.

Page 26-27, "Hist Whist," illustration from *Monster Soup* © 1992 Jacqueline Rogers. Art Director: Edith T. Weinberg.

Page 27, illustration from *Mathew Michael's Beastly Day* © 1992 Seymour Chwast. Art Director: Michael Farmer.

Page 28, cover illustration from *The Moon of the Winter Bird* © Vincent Nasta. Art Director: Al Cetta.

Page 29, illustration reprinted with permission of Atheneum Publishers, an imprint of Macmillan Publishing Company from *Taking Turns* by Bernice Wolman, illustrated by Catherine Stock. Illustrations © 1992 Catherine Stock. Art Director: Patrice Fodero.

Page 29, illustration reprinted with permission of Atheneum Publishers, an imprint of Macmillan Publishing Company from *Albert's Play* by Leslie Tryon. © 1992 Leslie Tryon. Art Director: Patrice Fodero.

Page 30, illustration by Kevin Hawkes from *His Royal Buckliness* © 1992 Kevin Hawkes. Reprinted by permission of Lothrop, Lee & Shepard Books, a division of William Morrow & Company, Inc. Art Director: Rachel Simon.

Page 30-31, jacket illustration from *The Cataract of Lodore* © 1992 David Catrow. Art Director: Maryann Leffingwell.

Page 31, illustration from *Jingle, the Christmas Clown* © 1992 Tomie dePaola. Art Director: Nanette Stevenson.

Page 32, illustration from *Who Shrank My Grandmother's House?* © Eric Beddows. Art Director: Al Cetta.

Page 32, illustration from *Square Triangle Round Skinny* © Eugenia and Vladimir Radunsky. Art Director: Maryann Leffingwell.

Page 33, illustration from *A Little Witch Magic* © 1992 Robert Bender. Art Director: Maryann Leffingwell.

Page 34, illustration from *On the Riverbank* © 1992 Melanie Hall. Art Director: Amy Bernstein.

Page 34-35, illustration from *Day Breaks* © Thomas Graham. Art

Director: Marc Cheshire.

Page 35, illustration from *Encounter* © 1992 David Shannon. Art Director: Michael Farmer. Designer: Lisa Peters.

Page 36, illustration from *Lucy's Winter Tale* © 1992 Troy Howell. Art Director: Atha Tehon.

Page 37, illustration from *The Boy Who Drew Cats* by David Johnson, © 1991 Rabbit Ears Productions, Inc. All rights reserved. Art Director: Motoko Inoue.

Page 37, illustration from *The Lost Sailor* © Richard Egielski. Art Director: Al Cetta.

Page 38, illustration by Paul Borovsky from *The Blabbermouths* by Gerda Mantinband. Illustrations © 1992 Paul Borovsky. Reprinted by permission of Greenwillow Books, a division of William Morrow & Company, Inc. Art Director: Ava Weiss.

Page 39, illustration by Victoria Chess from *Grim and Ghastly Goings-On* by Florence Parry Heide. Illustrations © 1992 Victoria Chess. Reprinted by permission of Lothrop, Lee & Shepard Books, a division of William Morrow & Company, Inc. Art Director: Rachel Simon.

Page 39, illustration from *The Changeling* © 1992 Jeanette Winter. Art Director: Denise Cronin. Designer: Edward Miller.

Page 40, illustration from *The Blacksmith and the Devils* © 1992 Maria Cristina Brusca. Art Director: Maryann Leffingwell.

Page 40, illustration from *Mean Soup* © 1991 Betsy Everitt. Art Director: Michael Farmer. Designer: Camilla Filancia.

Page 41, illustration from *Jane Yolen's Mother Goose Songbook* © 1992 Rosekrans Hoffman. Art Director: Joy Chu.

Page 42, illustration from *The Brave Little Tailor* © James Warhola. Art Director: Lucille Chomowicz.

Page 42-43, illustration from *Footprints and Shadows* © 1992 Henri Sorensen. Art Director: Lucille Chomowicz.

Page 43, illustration from *Petrouchka* © John Collier. Art Director: Alex Jay.

Page 44-45, illustration from *The Moon of the Salamanders* © 1992 Marlene Hill Werner. Art Director: Al Cetta.

Page 44-45, illustration from *The Wrong Side of the Bed*, written and illustrated by Wallace E. Keller, © 1992 Rizzoli International Publications. Art Director: Charles Kreloff.

Page 46, illustration from *Chester, The Out-of-Work Dog* © 1992 Cat Bowman Smith. Art Director: Maryann Leffingwell.

Page 46, illustration from *The Willow Pattern Story* © 1992 Allan Drummond. Art Director: Marc Cheshire.

Page 47, illustration from *The Snow Goose* © Beth Peck. Art Director: Denise Cronin.

Page 48, illustration by James Stevenson from his *Don't You Know There's a War On?* © 1992 James Stevenson. Reprinted by permission of Greenwillow Books, a division of William Morrow & Company, Inc. Art Director: Ava Weiss.

Page 48-49, illustration from *Circus* © 1992 Lois Ehlert. Art Director: Michael Farmer.

Page 49, illustration from *David's Songs* © Jerry Pinkney. Art Director: Atha Tehon.

Page 50, illustration by Anita Lobel from *Pierrot's ABC Garden*, © Anita Lobel. Art Director: Dave Werner.

Page 50-51, illustration from *Sami and the Time of the Troubles* © Ted Lewin. Art Director: Andrew Rhodes.

Page 51, illustration from *Moss Pillows* © Rosemary Wells. Art Director: Atha Tehon.

Page 52, illustration by Gennady Spirin reprinted by permission of Philomel Books from *Snow White & Rose Red* by Jakob and Wilhelm Grimm, illustrations © 1992 Gennady Spirin. Art Director: Nanette Stevenson.

Page 52, illustration by Nancy Tafuri from *Asleep, Asleep* by Mirra Ginsburg. Illustrations © 1992 Nancy Tafuri. Reprinted by permission of Greenwillow Books, a division of William Morrow & Company, Inc. Art Director: Ava Weiss.

Page 53, *Oink* poster illustration, © Arthur Geisert. Art Director: Amy Bernstein.

Page 53, illustration reprinted with permission of Atheneum Publishers, an imprint of Macmillan Publishing Company from *Mother Earth* by Nancy Luenn, illustrated by Neil Waldman. Illustrations © 1992 Neil Waldman. Art Director: Patrice Fodero.

Page 54, cover illustration reprinted with permission of Charles Scribner's Sons, an imprint of Macmillan Publishing Company from *The Golden Deer*, retold by Margaret Hodges, pictures by Daniel San Souci. Illustrations © 1992 Daniel San Souci. Art Director: Vikki Sheatsley.

Page 54-55, illustration from *Elijah's Angel* © 1992 Aminah Brenda Lynn Robinson. Art Director: Michael Farmer. Designer: Lucia D'moch.

Page 55, illustration from *Moe the Dog in Tropical Paradise* © 1992 Elise Primavera. Art Director: Nanette Stevenson.

Page 56, illustration from *The Folks in the Valley* © Stefano M. Vitale. Art Director: Al Cetta.

Page 57, illustration from *Old Black Fly* © 1992 Stephen Gammell. Art Director: Maryann Leffingwell.

Page 57, "The Coat, the Cat and the Monkey," illustration from *Hickory, Dickory, Dock* © Suzanne Duranceau. Art Director: Yuksel Hassan.

Page 58, illustration by Barry Root from *The Saint and the Circus* by Roberto Piumini. Illustrations © 1991 Barry Root. Reprinted by permission of Tambourine Books, a division of William Morrow & Company, Inc. Art Director: Golda Laurens.

Page 58, illustration by Heidi Goennel from *The Circus* © 1992 Heidi Goennel. Reprinted by permission of Tambourine Books, a division of William Morrow & Company, Inc. Art Director: Golda Laurens.

Page 59, illustration from *Moon of the Wild Pigs* © 1992 Paul Mirocha. Art Director: Al Cetta.

Page 60, illustration by Peter Sis from *An Ocean World* © 1992 Peter Sis. Reprinted by permission of Greenwillow Books, a division of William Morrow & Company, Inc. Art Director: Ava Weiss.

Page 60-61, illustration reprinted with permission of Bradbury Press, an affiliate of Macmillan, Inc. from *Petey Moroni's Camp Runamok Diary* by Pat Cummings. © 1992 Pat Cummings. Art Director: Julie Quan.

Page 61, illustration from *The Day Before Christmas* © 1992 Beth Peck. Art Director: Helene Berisky.

Page 62, cover illustration from *The Legend of Sleepy Hollow* © 1992 Michael Garland. Art Director: Tim Gillner. Designer: Charlotte Staub.

Page 62, illustration by Ed Young from *While I Sleep* by Mary Calhoun. Illustrations © 1992 Ed Young. Reprinted by permission of Morrow Junior Books, a division of William Morrow & Company, Inc. Art Director: Barbara Fitzsimmons.

Page 63, illustration from *Back Home* © Jerry Pinkney. Art Director: Atha Tehon.

Page 64, illustration by Maryjane Begin from *Little Mouse's Painting* by Diane Wolkstein. Illustrations © 1992 by Maryjane Begin. Reprinted by permission of Morrow Junior Books, a division of William Morrow & Company, Inc. Art Director: Barbara Fitzsimmons.

Page 64-65, illustration by Donald Crews from *Shortcut* © 1992 by Donald Crews. Reprinted by permission of Greenwillow Books, a division of William Morrow & Company, Inc. Art Director: Ava Weiss.

Page 65, illustration from *Chicken Sunday* © Patricia Polacco. Art Director: Nanette Stevenson. Designer: Nanette Stevenson.

Page 66, cover illustration from *The Girl Who Loved Caterpillars* © Floyd Cooper. Art Director: Nanette Stevenson.

Page 66, illustration from *One White Sail* © 1992 Lisa Etre. Art Director: Alan Benjamin.

Page 67, illustration reprinted with permission of Charles Scribner's Sons, an imprint of Macmillan Publishing Company from *Don Quixote and Sancho Panza* adapted by Margaret Hodges, illustrations by Stephen Marchesi. Illustrations © 1992 Stephen Marchesi. Art Director: Vikki Sheatsley.

Page 67, illustration from *On the Edge of the Sea* © Michael Paraskevas. Art Director: Atha Tehon.

Page 68, illustration reprinted with permission of Four Winds Press, an imprint of Macmillan Publishing Company from *Sukey and the Mermaid* by Robert D. San Souci, illustrated by Brian Pinkney. Illustrations © 1992 Brian Pinkney. Art Director: Christy Hale.

Page 68-69, illustration from *The Lion and the Little Red Bird* © 1992 Elisa Kleven. Art Director: Barbara Powderly.

Page 69, illustration from *Sing to the Sun* © 1992 Ashley Bryan. Art Director: Al Cetta.

Page 70, illustration from *Paper Boats* © Grayce Bochak. Art Director: Tim Gillner.

Page 70, illustration from *Boots & the Glass Mountain* © Gennady Spirin. Art Director: Atha Tehon.

Page 71, illustration from *Lost in the Amazon* © Robert Quackenbush. Art Director: Barbara Francis.

Page 71, illustration from *Jim Hedgehog and the Lonesome Tower* © Betsy Lewin. Art Director: Andrew Rhodes.

Page 72, "The Goat," illustration reprinted with permission of Margaret K. McElderry Books, an imprint of Macmillan Publishing Company from *The Beasts of Bethlehem* by X.J. Kennedy, illustrated by Michael McCurdy. Illustrations © 1992 Michael McCurdy. Art Director: Nancy Williams.

Page 72, illustration from *Zomo the Rabbit* © 1992 Gerald McDermott. Art Director: Michael Farmer.

Page 73, illustration from *Little Love Song* © Petra Mathers. Art Director: Denise Cronin.

Page 74, illustration reprinted with permission of Four Winds Press, an imprint of Macmillan Publishing Company from *Sofie's Role* by Amy Heath, illustrated by Sheila Hamanaka. Illustrations © 1992 Sheila Hamanaka. Art Director: Christy Hale.

Page 74, illustration from *Seeing Eye Willie* © Dale Gottlieb. Art Director: Denise Cronin. Designer: Edward Miller.

Page 75, illustration from *Daffy Down Dillies* © 1992 John O'Brien. Art Director: Jeanne Krulis. Designer: Katy Riegel.

Page 75, illustration from *A Grandmother's Story* © Glenn Halak, published by Green Tiger Press/Simon & Schuster 1992. Art Director: Alan Benjamin.

Page 76, illustration by Lindsay Barrett George from *Christmas at Long Pond* by William T. George. Illustrations © 1992 Lindsay Barrett George. Reprinted by permission of Greenwillow Books, a division of William Morrow & Company, Inc. Art Director: Ava Weiss.

Page 76-77, "Subway Delay," illustration from *Sam Panda and Thunder Dragon* © 1992 Chris Conover. Art Director: Cynthia Krupat.

Page 77, illustration from *Grandma's Latkes* © 1992 Eve Chwast. Art Director: Michael Farmer. Designer: Lisa Peters.

Page 78, cover illustration from *Maggie Mab and the Bogey Beast* © 1992 Johanna Westerman. Art Director: Marc Cheshire.

Page 78, illustration from *Tomato Soup* © 1992 Thacher Hurd. Art Director: John Grandits.

Page 79, "Hey Tapple Tapple...," illustration reprinted with permission of Atheneum Publishers, an imprint of Macmillan Publishing Company from *The Cat & the Fiddle & More* by Jim Aylesworth, illustrated by Richard Hull. Illustrations © 1992 Richard Hull. Art Director: Patrice Fodero.

Page 80, illustration from *An Island Christmas* © 1991 Catherine Stock. Art Director: Andrew Rhodes.

Page 80-81, illustration by Maggie Smith from *My Grandma's Chair* © 1992 Margaret C. Smith. Reprinted by permission of Lothrop, Lee & Shepard Books, a division of William Morrow & Company, Inc. Art Director: Rachel Simon.

Page 81, illustration from *Working Cotton* © Carole Byard. Art Director: Michael Farmer. Designer: Trina Stahl.

Page 82, illustration from *Whoo-oo Is It?* © 1992 S.D. Schindler. Designer: Mina Greenstein.

Page 82, cover illustration from *Wolf Plays Alone* © 1992 Dominic Catalano. Art Director: Nanette Stevenson.

Page 83, illustration by Anita Lobel from *This Quiet Lady* by Charlotte Zolotow. Illustrations © 1992 Anita Lobel. Art Director: Ava Weiss. Reprinted by permission of Greenwillow Books, a division of William Morrow & Company, Inc.

Page 84, illustration by Friso Henstra from *Cynthia and the Runaway Gazebo* © 1992 Friso Henstra. Reprinted by permission of Tambourine Books, a division of William Morrow & Company, Inc. Art Director: Golda Laurens.

Page 84, illustration from *Train Leaves the Station* © Dale Gottlieb. Art Director: Maryann Leffingwell. A Bill Martin Book.

Page 85, illustration from *A Coney Tale* © 1992 Paul Rátz de Tagyos. Art Director: Andrew Rhodes.

Page 86, "Christmas Safari," illustration from *Oscar de Mejo's ABC* © Oscar de Mejo. Art Director: Al Cetta. From the collection of Nahan Galleries, New Orleans. Courtesy Dorothy de Mejo.

Page 87, illustration from *Trees,* © 1992 James Endicott. Art Director: Bill Martin.

Page 87, illustration from *The Nutcracker Ballet* illustrated by Stephen J. Johnson © 1992 Andrews and McMeel. Art Director: Rick Cusick.

Page 88, illustration from *Pumpkins* © Barrett Root. Art Director: Michael Farmer.

Page 88, illustration from *Father and Son* © 1992 Jonathan Green. Art Director: Nanette Stevenson. Designer: Gunta Alexander.

Page 89, illustration from *Little Fish, Big Fish* © 1993 Frank Asch. Art Director: Edith T. Weinberg. Designer: Laurie McBarnette.

Page 90, illustration by Arden Johnson from *The Sleepytime Book* by Jan Wahl. Illustrations © 1992 Arden Johnson. Reprinted by permission of Tambourine Books, a division of William Morrow & Company, Inc. Art Director: Golda Laurens.

Page 90-91, illustration from *Sweet Dreams, Willy* © 1992 Lizi Boyd. Art Director: Cecilia Yung.

Page 91, illustration from *But No Candy* © Lloyd Bloom. Art Director: Nanette Stevenson.

Page 92, illustration from *Lucky Russell* © Bradley D. Sneed. Art Director: Patrick Collins.

Page 92, illustration from *The Giraffe That Walked to Paris* © 1992 Roger Roth. Art Director: Isabel Warren-Lynch.

Page 93, illustration from *The Fool and the Flying Ship* by Henrik Drescher, © 1992 Rabbit Ears Productions, Inc. Art Directors: Paul Elliot and Motoko Inoue. All rights reserved.

Page 94, illustration from *The Great Pumpkin Switch* © 1992 Ted Lewin. Art Director: Mina Greenstein.

Page 94-95, illustration from *Look Out, Look Out, It's Coming!* © 1992 Susan G. Truesdell. Art Director: Al Cetta.

Page 95, illustration from *The Twelve Days of Christmas* © Dorothée Duntze. Art Director: Marc Cheshire.

Page 96, illustration from *The Samurai's Daughter* © Stephen T.

Johnson. Art Director: Atha Tehon.

Page 97, illustration from *A Farmyard Song* © 1992 Christopher Manson. Art Director: Marc Cheshire.

Page 97, illustration from *East of the Sun, West of the Moon* © 1992 Rabbit Ears Productions, Inc. All rights reserved. Art Directors: Paul Elliot and Motoko Inoue.

Page 98, illustration from *The Heart of the Wood* © 1992 Sheila Hamanaka. Art Director: Lucille Chomowicz.

Page 98, illustration from *Matreshka* © 1992 Alexi Natchev. Art Director: Lynn Braswell.

Page 99, illustration from *Evil Under the Sea* © Robert Quackenbush. Art Director: Barbara Francis.

Page 100, "The Elephant," illustration from *A Zooful of Animals* © Lynn Munsinger. Art Director: Walter Lorraine.

Page 100, illustration from *Themba* © 1992 Wil Clay. Art Director: Rosemary Brosnan.

Page 101, illustration from *Drylongso* © Jerry Pinkney. Art Director: Michael Farmer. Designer: Trina Stahl.

Page 101, illustration from *Bigfoot and Other Legendary Creatures* © William Noonan Art Director: Michael Farmer.

Page 102, illustration from *Why the Sky Is Far Away* © Carla Golembe. Art Director: Susan Lu.

Page 103, illustration from *Morning Milking* © 1991 David DeRan. Art Director: Robert Saunders.

Page 103, illustration from *Orpheus* © Charles Mikolaycak, courtesy Harcourt Brace Jovanovich. Art Director: Michael Farmer.

Page 104, illustration from *The Leaving Morning* © David Soman. Art Director: Mina Greenstein.

Page 104-05, illustration reprinted with permission of Macmillan Publishing Company from *Matthew Wheelock's Wall* by Frances Ward Weller. Illustrations © 1992 Ted Lewin. Art Director: Jeanne Krulis.

Page 105, "Yellow Crowned Night Heron," illustration from *Wings Along the Waterway* © 1992 Mary Barrett Brown. Art Director: Alice Lee Groton.

Page 106, illustration from *The Elephant's Wrestling Match* © Brian Pinkney. Designer: Marilyn Granald.

Page 106, illustration from *Bambi* © 1992 Michael J. Woods. Art Director: Lucille Chomowicz. Designer: Vicki Kalajian.

Page 107, illustration from *One Day, Two Dragons* © 1992 Janet Street. Art Director: Howard Klein.

Page 108, illustration from *What Do You Like?* © 1992 Michael Grejniec. Art Director: Marc Cheshire. Designer: Michael Grejniec.

Page 108, illustration from *First Tomato* © Rosemary Wells. Art Director: Atha Tehon.

Page 109, "Tantrum," illustration from the book *Antics!* © 1992 Catherine Hepworth. Art Director: Nanette Stevenson.

Page 110, illustration by Steve Johnson from *Up North at the Cabin* by Marsha Wilson Chall. Illustrations © 1992 Steve Johnson. Reprinted by permission of Lothrop, Lee & Shepard Books, a division of William Morrow & Company, Inc. Art Director: Lou Fancher.

Page 110, illustration reprinted with permission of Macmillan Publishing Company from *Boris the Boring Boar* by Ellen Jackson, illustrated by Normand Chartier. Illustrations © 1992 Normand Chartier. Art Directors: Cecilia Yung and Jeanne Krulis.

Page 111, illustration from *The Finest Horse in Town* © 1992 Susan Gaber. Art Director: Harriett Barton.

Page 111, illustration from *The Old Man and the Fiddle* © 1992 Michael McCurdy. Art Director: Gunta Alexander.

Page 112, illustration from *The Escape of Marvin the Ape* © 1992 Mark Buehner. Art Director: Atha Tehon. Designer: Mara Nussbaum.

Page 112, illustration from *The Old Red Rocking Chair* © 1992 John Sandford. Art Director: Marc Cheshire.

Page 113, illustration from *Itchy, Itchy Chickenpox* © Betsy Lewin. Art Director: Edith T. Weinberg.

Page 113, illustration from *Peter's Song* © Diane deGroat. Art Director: Sylvia Frezzolini. Designer: Vicki Kalajian.

Page 114, illustration from *The Simple People* © 1992 Andrew Shachat. Art Director: Atha Tehon.

Page 114, illustration from *The Broody Hen* © 1992 Olivier Dunrea. Art Director: Cecilia Yung.

Page 115, illustration from *Sir Whong and the Golden Pig* © 1992 Oki S. Han. Art Director: Atha Tehon.

Page 115, illustration reprinted with permission of Macmillan Publishing Company from *My River* by Shari Halpern. Copyright © 1992 Shari Halpern. Art Director: Jean Krulis.

Page 116, illustration from *In the Eyes of the Cat* © 1992 Demi. Art Director: Maryann Leffingwell.

Page 116-17, illustration from *June 29, 1999* © David Wiesner. Art Director: Carol Goldenberg.

Page 117, illustration from *Mrs. Katz and Tush* © Patricia Polacco. Art Director: Marla Martin.

Page 118, illustration from *The Tiger and the Brahmin* by Kurt Vargö © 1992 Rabbit Ears Productions, Inc. All rights reserved. Art Directors: Paul Elliot, Motoko Inoue.

Page 119, illustration from *Jack and the Beanstalk* by Edward Sorel, © 1991 Rabbit Ears Productions, Inc. All rights reserved. Art Directors: Paul Elliot and Motoko Inoue.

Page 119, illustration by Janet Street from *Dinosaur Dress Up* by Allen L. Sirois. Illustrations © 1992 Janet Street. Reprinted by permission of Tambourine Books, a division of William Morrow & Company, Inc. Art Director: Golda Laurens.

Page 120, illustration from *Messiah* © Barry Moser. Art Directors: Barry Moser and Al Cetta.

Page 121, "Whale and Dolphins," illustration from *It's My Earth, Too* © 1992 Melanie Hope Greenberg. Art Director: Lynn Braswell.

Page 121, illustration from *Rainflowers* © 1992 Robert J. Blake. Art Director: Harriett Barton.

Page 122, illustration © Samuel Byrd. Reprinted from *Let Freedom Ring: A Ballad of Martin Luther King, Jr.* Art Director: Tere LoPrete. By permission of Holiday House, Inc.

Page 123, illustration from *Spacey Riddles* © 1992 Simms Taback. Art Director: Atha Tehon.

Page 123, "That Is How Pigs Go to Sleep," illustration from *Going to Sleep on the Farm* © Juan Wijngaard. Art Director: Atha Tehon.

Page 124, illustration from *Emily and the Crows* © Elaine Greenstein. Art Director: Robert Saunders.

Page 124, illustration from *Moon Rope* © 1992 Lois Ehlert. Art Director: Michael Farmer.

Page 125, illustration from *Mister Toad* © 1992 N. Cameron Watson. Art Director: Jean Krulis.

Page 125, illustration from *Dinosaur for a Day* © Mark Alan Weatherby. Art Director: Claire Counihan.

Page 126, illustration from *The Walloping Window-Blind* © Ted Rand. Art Director: Marc Cheshire.

Page 126, illustration from *The Animal That Drank Up Sound* © Debra Frasier. Art Director: Michael Farmer.

Page 127, illustration from *Klara's New World* © 1992 Jeanette Winter. Art Director: Denise Cronin.

Page 128, illustration from *Eeny, Meeny, Miney Mole* © 1992 Kathryn Brown. Art Director: Michael Farmer.

Page 128, illustration from *The Professor of Etiquette* © Oscar de Mejo. Courtesy Dorothy de Mejo.

Page 129, illustration from *The Hidden Jungle* © 1992 Simon Henwood. Art Director: Martha Rago.

Page 129, illustration from *Hugh Can Do* © Kimberly Bulcken Root. Art Director: Isabel Warren-Lynch.

Index of Illustrators

Index of Authors